THE BREVIARY AND THE LAITY

By the Reverend
RODOLPHE HOORNAERT

Catholic Authors Press
www.CatholicAuthors.com

NIHIL OBSTAT
VIRGILIUS MICHEL, O.S.B.
Censor Deputatus

IMPRIMI POTEST
✠ ALCUINUS DEUTSCH, O.S.B.
Abbas S. Joannis Bapt

IMPRIMATUR
✠ JOSEPHUS F. BUSCH
Episcopus S. Clodoaldi

S. Clodoaldi, die 18. Aprilis, A.D. 1936

First published 1936
Reprinted 2007 Catholic Authors Press

ISBN: 978-0-9783198-1-6

Catholic Authors Press

www.CatholicAuthors.org

TRANSLATORS' NOTE

It is not by mere accident but by design that this booklet appears in English translation coincidently with the formation of the League of the Divine Office which is sponsored by the liturgical apostolate of St. John's Abbey through its monthly review, *Orate Fratres.* The increasing interest of layfolk in the Breviary is evidence of the advance of liturgical revival throughout the country. As *Orate Fratres* nears the tenth anniversary of its own foundation, it is able to launch this effort toward an objective which ten years ago seemed to many beyond reasonable hope of attainment.

While this booklet is addressed directly to the laity, it renders service also to the clergy and religious. There is significance in the fact that the present translation is a product of work done by a group of seminarians of the St. Paul Seminary in their course of Breviary studies.

The author is known to English readers through his writings on St. Teresa (Sheed and Ward) and on St. John of the Cross (Burns Oates). In the present booklet he has contrived to present much valuable material within a small compass. In pleading for the use of the Breviary by layfolk he is careful not to ask for more than given circumstances permit. And in pursuing his theme throughout the various stages of prayer-life, he displays the values contained in the divine Office for the profit both of beginners and of those more advanced.

WILLIAM BUSCH

The St. Paul Seminary

CONTENTS

PAGE

Translators' Note v

Preface ix

Introduction 13

Part I. The Breviary and Vocal Prayer 19

Part II. The Breviary and Discursive Prayer 40

Part III. The Breviary and Affective Prayer 64

Part IV. The Breviary and Contemplative Prayer 81

Appendix:

    Outline of the Office 109

    General Remarks on the Use of the Breviary ... 115

    Sample Outlines 115

PREFACE

It may seem a bold statement to say that the recitation of the Breviary affords a method of prayer capable of conducting the soul from first steps in the spiritual life to the most exalted degrees of the contemplative state. Yet such is the opinion maintained by the Abbé Rodolphe Hoornaert in this booklet which proposes that the Breviary be again put into the hands of the laity.

It is a rather astonishing proposal, for, at present, while the Breviary is recited by all priests and by many members of religious communities, very few of the laity are acquainted with it. Nor is this a surprising fact. In order to pray the Breviary it is necessary to overcome certain prejudices and to make a considerable effort. It is so much easier to take up one of the books prepared for popular devotion, to pick out certain prayers according to one's preference, and to meditate upon them according to a ready-made plan in which the points follow along in a certain logical order.

Would not a return to the freer method based on the official formulas of liturgical prayer imply a disregard for the accumulated experiences represented in the various modern systems of prayer which certainly have contributed to the spiritual formation of many people?

And yet, as the author explains very correctly, in the great ages of the faith the Breviary was, along with the Missal, the spiritual storehouse from which the piety of all the faithful was sustained. It is quite true that for many centuries the only manuals of devotion were the liturgical books, with, of course, the sacred Scriptures and the writings of the Fathers. It is only since the fifteenth century that these books were gradually neglected in favor of new treatises on Christian spirituality.

We must recognize, however, that the idea of using the Breviary as a "manual of piety" will encounter various objections. Our author takes these into consideration and meets them directly. To recite the Breviary with real spiritual profit a considerable amount of time must be given to it. Do we actually lack the time; or do we perhaps not employ our time properly? And if actually our time must be engaged with other things, can we not recite at least some part of the Breviary if the whole of it is out of question? The fact that one does not know Latin is not a serious obstacle, for translations are available.

On the other hand, what great advantages are derived from the recitation of the divine Office! The principal one, no doubt, is this, that it enables us to live a truly liturgical life, since it keeps us always in contact with the life of Christ our Lord in the Church which is His mystical body. Reciting the psalms intelligently and devoutly, we participate directly in the vital movements of that organism which continually receives a divine influx proceeding from Christ its head.

In regard to meditation and contemplation there may seem to be some question. From the point of view of modern piety, we are inclined to think that meditation must necessarily be conceived as a methodical exercise in which one strives to extract by study the spiritual value contained in some truth or mystery. Is this rather formal procedure actually suitable for everyone? Does it appeal effectively to every sort of mind and will? The more liberal method which our author advocates and which is followed by most of our monastic orders, makes meditation and contemplation to be the logical consequence of vocal prayer, a prolongation of vocal prayer into the high region of intimate contact with God. From this point of view may not the Breviary be the very best book of meditation?

We can only invite the reader to try out the procedure which the author suggests in this booklet. He points out practical ways in which the vocal prayer of the Breviary may be carried over into meditation and into the higher realm of contemplation. The reader will be astonished and amazed to discover in the Breviary a wealth unsuspected by the majority of Christians, and will bless Heaven at being able to nourish his devotion from this same divine source which supplies the clergy with vigor for their priestly life.

"The book written within and without," is not this a beautiful description of the Breviary, which is indeed a sequel to the sacred Scriptures?

"*Tolle et lege*—take and read, open, and pray and ponder." Thus says the interior voice which invites the Christian to take up the Breviary and to find in it the ways of true piety.

☩ THEODORE NEVE,
Abbot of St. Andrew.

Abbey of St. Andrew,
Lophem-lez-Bruges, Belgium,
October 5, 1934.

INTRODUCTION

The Church has her official books of prayer. They are the Missal, the Breviary, the Ritual, the Pontifical and the Ceremonial of Bishops.

The most important of these, as regards the laity, are certainly the Missal and the Breviary, although every educated Catholic should have some knowledge of the Ritual, which contains the beautiful prayers for a large part of the Church's sacramental administration, and the Pontifical and Ceremonial, which contain such solemn rites as the ordination of priests and the consecration of churches.

Some thirty years ago our Catholic layfolk had hardly any knowledge of these books. They have by now come to know the Missal and it is being used by ever-growing numbers. But the other liturgical books are still strange to them. It is our hope that what has been realized in the case of the Missal may also be realized, of course in due proportion, in the case of the Breviary; that at least our educated Catholics, and in some degree all our people, may profit by contact with this second source of liturgical piety.

In these pages we shall try to show that the divine Office is indeed an inexhaustible source of spiritual life, not only for those who are obliged to it by their state, but for all the faithful.

With the Breviary in hand we propose to consider the various degrees of prayer, corresponding to the several stages of the spiritual life, namely: 1) vocal prayer, 2) discursive prayer or meditation, 3) affective prayer, and 4) contemplative prayer, and to show how wonderfully the divine Office meets the needs of the soul in all these stages.

But first of all, there are certain general ideas that must be grasped at the start:

I. Definition:

The Breviary is the liturgical book which contains the formulas of prayer by which the Church daily and unceasingly renders praise to God.

It is made up of four volumes, corresponding to the four seasons of the year: winter, spring, summer and autumn.

The word "Breviary" comes from the Latin *breviarium* and means an abridgment, a reduction into more convenient form of the various books (psalter, antiphonary, hymnal etc.) which were used in former times in the recitation or chant of the divine Office, which itself was considerably abbreviated in the twelfth and thirteenth centuries.[1]

II. Composition:

Each volume of the Breviary is made up of the following parts (after an introduction which contains especially the calendar and certain general directions or "rubrics"):

1) The Ordinary: *i.e.*, the elements which recur daily in the Office and which determine its general pattern.

2) The Psalter: *i.e.*, the one hundred fifty psalms distributed over the seven days of the week, and which with their antiphons are to be introduced at their assigned place in the daily Office.

3) The Proper: *i.e.*, including those parts of the Office which belong to each separate day and which recur only once a year. The Proper is subdivided into:

[1] Callewaert, *De Brevarii Romani Liturgia*, p. 3, and note 13.

a) *The Temporal*: *i.e.*, the proper parts for each day of the liturgical seasons.

b) *The Sanctoral*: *i.e.*, the proper parts for the various saints'-days.

4) The Common of the Saints: *i.e.*, the parts assigned to the various classes of saints.

5) An Appendix: containing the Office of the Dead, the Little Office of the Blessed Virgin, and various prayers in frequent use but not strictly part of the Office.

III. Classification:

The entire content of the Breviary is called the divine Office or the ecclesiastical Office.

Although the general structure of the Office is the same for every day, there are some differences which may be shown in the following classification:

I. The Dominical or Sunday Office:

A. *Major*:

    a) of the first class: *e.g.*, the First Sunday of Advent;

    b) of the second class: *e.g.*, Septuagesima Sunday.

B. *Minor*: *e.g.*, the Twentieth Sunday after Pentecost.

II. The Ferial or Week Day Office:

A. *Major*:

    a) Privileged: *e.g.*, Ash Wednesday;

    b) Non-privileged: *e.g.*, a week day in Advent.

B. *Minor*: *e.g.*, any ordinary week day.

III. The Festival or Saints'-Day Office:

A. *Double*:
1) of the first class:
   a) primary: *e.g.*, Christmas;
   b) secondary: *e.g.*, Sacred Heart;
2) of the second class:
   a) primary: *e.g.*, an Apostle;
   b) secondary: *e.g.*, Finding of the Cross,
3) major:
   a) primary: *e.g.*, St. Augustine;
   b) secondary: *e.g.*, Exaltation of the Cross;
4) minor: *e.g.*, St. Walburga.

B. *Semi-double*: *e.g.*, St. Louis.

C. *Simple*: *e.g.*, St. Evaristus.

N. B. Besides the various Offices indicated in this table, there are other types that occur less frequently, such as: the Offices of Vigils and Octaves, the Office of the Blessed Virgin on Saturday, the Office of the Dead.

To assist layfolk in finding their way in the Breviary we shall offer in the appendix of this booklet several typical outlines. These should be studied carefully.

IV. Character:

The term "Office" comes from the Latin word *officium*, which means *duty*. The recitation of this prayer is indeed a duty; for it is the duty of all creation to praise the Creator daily and unceasingly. The Church undertakes to fulfil this obligation by means of those who are deputed and dedicated to this purpose, priests, monks and nuns.

These have concluded a solemn pledge with the Church to maintain constantly the sacred flame of divine psalmody. They are the voice of the Church by thousands.

The Breviary contains the text of this divine worship. Its characteristic note, that which makes the prayer of the Breviary noticeably different from the prayer of various other books, is this, that it is essentially prayer of praise. The Church's official prayer is chiefly in the form of praise and thanksgiving.

Breviary prayer proclaims the beauty of God, His goodness, majesty and might. For the sake of His praise it speaks of the life and virtues of the saints. And yet it does not omit to beseech His majesty for all our spiritual and temporal needs.

The Breviary is the Church's own composition. But it is made up for the most part from the words of the Holy Spirit taken from the sacred Scriptures.

This worship of God is to go on day by day without interruption. It is perpetual as regards both time and place; throughout all time, for it dates back to the very beginning of the Church, if not in its precise present form at least in its general substance; and in every place, for it goes on in every part of the world, wherever there is a priest, wherever there is one whom the Church has dedicated to this function of divine praise.

Surely a beautiful thing! Everywhere the same doctrine, the same Missal and Ritual and Breviary, one voice of praise throughout the world, uniting with the eternal chorus of heaven. Who is there with a sense of catholicity that would not wish to take part, some part at least, in this great catholic prayer?

PART ONE

THE BREVIARY AS A MANUAL OF VOCAL PRAYER

I. Objections:

In whatever way these may be worded, they may be reduced to the following heads, and are usually conceived from a practical point of view:

1) I have not the time.
2) I am not a priest or a monk or nun, and besides I do not wish to appear ridiculous.
3) I have no knowledge of Latin.
4) The Missal is enough for me; at most I might perhaps consider the addition of Vespers.

II. The question in the light of history:

a) *In the first Christian centuries*:

The divine Office arose out of the Vigil service. The early Christians assembled on Saturday evening and kept watch until dawn, during which time they sang "psalms, hymns and spiritual canticles," and listened to the reading of passages from the Scriptures or from the letters of the apostles. The meeting ended on Sunday morning with the celebration of the eucharistic Sacrifice.

b) *From the fourth to the sixth centuries*:

During this period the prayer books contained the psalms of the Old Testament and Christian hymns and doxologies. The Church did not provide any other prayer books for layfolk. St. Ambrose, speaking of the psalter, says that it is a book which daybreak should always find in the hands of a virgin. By this time certain other prayers had been added and the number went on increasing; these are the "orations" or collects as we have them in the Missal.

c) *In the Middle Ages*:

We still find the laity using the prayers of the Office. Those who were able to read used the Book of the Hours, a more or less complete edition of the Office. There are examples of such books of the Hours, as used by layfolk, in richly illuminated copies, such as the "Heures Riches" of the Duke of Berry, the Breviary of Philip the Good, the Grimani Breviary, etc. In the life of St. Elizabeth of Hungary we read how in her childhood she was wont to pray in the chapel of the castle, a little girl with a huge breviary. Joinville in his life of St. Louis IX tells us how this good king "made his sons learn the Hours of our Lady and had them read the Day Hours in his presence in order to form in them the habit of assisting at the Hours in future days when they would rule their own territories."

d) *In the Renaissance period*, fifteenth and sixteenth centuries:

The Books of the Hours continued in use among the laity. But a change becomes noticeable in the orientation of popular piety. Layfolk tend increasingly to neglect the recitation of the Hour-prayers.

Causes of this decline:

1. The individualistic spirit of Protestantism and, later, of the eighteenth century. Popular piety among Catholics was influenced to some extent by the Protestant spirit

and there appeared an increasing tendency toward individualism in prayer.

2. Ignorance of Latin among ordinary layfolk. Knowledge of Latin was still rather widespread at the beginning of the fifteenth century, but now began to die out. The modern languages assert their independence. The sciences have begun to employ the vernacular, and spiritual literature tends the same way although at a slower pace.

3. The educated laity conceive a distaste for medieval Latin as inferior to the classical. Humanism finds it unbearable. This is the period in which the bishop, Zacharias Ferreri, disfigures the Breviary with illusions to pagan mythology and introduces Venus and Bacchus into the hymns.

4. The continual changes introduced in the composition of the Breviary and the abuses promoted by the Franciscans who made the Breviary a burden by adding all sorts of prayers and supplementary Offices. It all became so complicated that the laity were inclined to leave to monks and priests the task of disentangling it.

e) *In the seventeenth and eighteenth centuries*:

The idea of popular participation in the Office persists in some measure despite all. This is the golden age of the *Officiola*, little offices, reduced in size but patterned after the Office itself, and adapted to the needs of private piety, which latter nevertheless prevailed more and more.[1]

f) *In modern times*:

Thus there appear in the nineteenth century those pathetic formulas in which certain extracts of the divine Office still survive: Vespers for Sundays, the Seven Penitential Psalms, the Little Office of the Blessed Virgin.

---

[1] On the *Officiola* see the article of G. Malherbe in the *Bulletin Paroissial Liturgique*, 1934, n. 2, 3, 4.

In recent times the use of the Missal has reawakened interest in many parts of the Breviary. The Missal calls for the Breviary as its complement. Nevertheless, in regard to the Breviary we are still just where we were thirty years ago in regard to the Missal.

III. Reply to objections:

1) *I have not the time*:

This objection is generally not admissable. If anyone will only examine his daily routine and consider the many things for which he does manage to find time, he will discover that it is possible to make a number of useful substitutions, if it be only in order to give the first place in his life to spiritual things.

Moreover, even without any such substitutions, it is possible to gain time simply by less waste of it in idle conversations. By diminishing a little one's converse with men it will be possible to converse a little more with God. Of course outward undertakings are profitable, but they might perhaps be all the more so if we would spend less time in talking about them and more time in praying for them.

If actually you have not time enough to recite the entire Office (which is quite likely the case with most people), you can still recite some part of it: Matins only, or just the lessons of Matins, or simply Prime and Compline as morning and evening prayers, or Vespers, or Compline each evening.

If this cannot be done daily, you can at least select some day when you have more leisure, Sunday for example.

2) *I am not a priest or religious*:

Where and at what time in history did the Church ever say that the Missal and Breviary are intended exclusively for priests and monks and nuns? It is true that they are the delegated functionaries in the Church's official prayer. They have made this their vocation and have freely contracted the obligation. But does the existence of a standing army in any nation prevent the citizens generally from enrolling as volunteers?

Thus in regard to the official prayer of the Church, the only difference between clergy and laity is that the former are appointed to this function in virtue of their mission and are bound to it under penalty, whereas the interest of the laity is quite voluntary. It would indeed be a sad thing if those whom the Church does not actually oblige to take part in the chorus of divine praise were to take no interest in it, leaving it altogether to those officially appointed. As on the other hand it would be distressing to think that the latter perform their task only because obliged to it under penalty.

The Church never intended that there should be two kinds of piety and two forms of prayer, one for the clergy and another for the laity. There is simply the prayer of the Church. One prays with the Church and as the Church does, or else outside the Church or alongside the Church.

3) *I have no knowledge of Latin:*

This is indeed a disadvantage, for one misses many things in consequence. The language of the Church in the western world is Latin. People are ready enough to learn several or all the European languages if it will help them in business. Should we not be willing to learn only this one for the sake of the spiritual advantages which it will enable us to enjoy?

However, knowledge of Latin is not indispensable in order to use the Breviary, no more than it is for the Missal, since the text may be had in translations.[1]

4) *The Missal keeps me sufficiently in contact with the official prayer of the Church:*

No, the Missal is not enough and it would be a mistake to think so. The Missal and Breviary go together and each completes the other. If those who love the Mass wish to carry their devotion to its logical conclusion, they must inevitably take up the Breviary. The Office is at once a preparation for the Mass and a prolongation of it. If therefore the Missal has taught you to understand the Mass as the Church does, why not also make use of the Church's official preparation for Mass (First Vespers, Matins and Lauds), and why not continue throughout the day to dwell with the Church upon the theme of the morning Mass (in the Minor Hours, Second Vespers and Compline)?

There is, moreover, a close correspondence in the content of these two books. The theme for each day is the same in both of them, the same mystery or the same saint of the day. The collect of the Mass for a given day appears also as the oration in Lauds, the Minor Hours and Vespers. On days when the Mass is celebrated in honor of some saint, an account of such one's life is read in the second nocturn of Matins. The lessons of the first nocturn often correspond to the epistle of the Mass, which latter again is broken up into brief passages for the short les-

---

[1] Prime and Compline are published in English in pamphlet form by the Liturgical Press, Collegeville, Minn. There is an English edition of the Day Hours (including all except Matins) published by Burns Oates & Washbourne, London. A complete English edition of the Breviary is in preparation and is soon to be published by the same firm.

sons of the Minor Hours. The homily lessons of the third nocturn are a commentary on the gospel of the Mass. Thus in order to follow out the Mass completely one must recite the Breviary; and hence in brief: the Missal calls for the Breviary.

IV. Positive advantages:

Thus far we have answered objections. Let us now consider some of the advantages to be derived from the recitation of the Breviary.

1. To unite with the priest every day at the holy sacrifice of the Mass by means of the Missal, and to unite every day with priests the world over and with the supreme Pontiff in the unity of the whole Church by means of the Breviary, is to follow out the complete cycle and to lead a thoroughly liturgical life.

2. To use the Breviary in preference to books of private prayer, is truly to establish a new bond of union with Christ as our High-priest and with His Church, to be of one voice with the Bridegroom and Bride, to speak their language and not a foreign one. And it matters little in this respect whether it be in Latin or in English.

3. You will discover that the Breviary provides the usual forms of prayer to which you are attached. You will find that your own sentiments and your own intentions are not overlooked.

a) We shall observe later on that the Breviary includes morning and evening prayers, beautiful prayers of thanksgiving, of contrition and penance, of anguish in times of trial, of petition for all one's needs.

b) The four motives of all prayer are present in the Office as in the Mass, namely: adoration, thanksgiving, reparation and petition. The office renders homage to God and at the same time brings blessing to us. It is profitable first of all to the entire Church, since we pray both with and for the Church, and indeed for the whole universe. This is the *general* fruit of the Office. And next, the Church prescribes certain intentions and so bids us pray, *e.g.*, for the faithful departed, for the Pope and hierarchy and clergy and for all the people. These are the *special* fruits of the Office. But furthermore, we are expected to add our own private intentions, *e.g.*, the obtaining of some particular grace, the conversion of some sinner, the cure of some illness, the success of an undertaking. These are the *very special* fruits of the Office.

4. Whatever our particular intentions may be, our prayer will prove more efficacious when united with that of the Church, for it will rise before the divine majesty as a part of the great choral prayer of those who are dedicated to this service in the mystical body of Christ.

5. The recitation of the Breviary keeps one in daily contact with the sacred Scriptures and with the Catholic tradition in a greater degree than does the Missal alone. How many educated Catholics know but little of the Scriptures and the writings of the Fathers. Non-Catholics have often reproached us on this score, and what have we to say in reply?

6. Finally, recitation of the Breviary by layfolk will keep them in close contact with the clergy. People often complain about the monotony of sermons. Certainly these might be elevated to a higher plane if both priests and people would seek information and inspiration from the same sources. If priests were able to speak according to the Missal and Breviary to people acquainted with these same books, there would be no lack of elevated thought in their sermons. It is sometimes argued that in our liturgical serv-

ices the clergy ought to use the language of the people. We are not concerned here to enter into this debate. But, to turn the subject about, why not argue that the people ought to acquire some knowledge of the priest's language, if not literally, at least some knowledge of its thought as expressed in a translation?

Moreover, if a priest finds that the people are interested in the Office, whether they recite it regularly or assist attentively at public recitation, he will be the more inclined to recite it well himself and to guard himself against any negligence.

Recitation of the Breviary offers to layfolk an opportunity to render service, in a simple and modest and unpretentious way, as auxiliaries to the clergy. Some priests are so over-burdened in the work of the ministry that they are hardly able to give to the Office the full amount of attention and devotion that they would wish. Those of the laity who may have more leisure may well volunteer therefore to undertake a careful recitation of the Office so that God may not be deprived of the homage which He deserves.

V. Practical applications:

Having thus presented our argument, we shall proceed to enforce it by examples taken from the Breviary, and we shall group these in the order of the four following propositions:

1. The Breviary includes all of the four chief kinds of prayer (*i.e.*, according to motive), namely: prayer of adoration, of thanksgiving, of propitiation (*i.e.*, of contrition and penance) and of impetration (*i.e.*, of petition for spiritual or temporal goods).

a) *Prayer of adoration:*

The Breviary abounds in wonderful formulas of adoration and praise. Indeed this high motive is the one that appears most frequently. Is this the reason why the laity have lost contact with the Breviary? Does this motive fail to interest the general run of men? Far be it from us to think so.

Examples:

At the end of every psalm comes the beautiful formula of praise addressed to the Holy Trinity: "Glory be to the Father and to the Son and to the Holy Ghost."

At the end of Matins comes the magnificent doxology, the *Te Deum*: "We praise Thee, O God; we acknowledge Thee to be the Lord; heaven and earth are full of the majesty of Thy glory; the holy Church throughout the world doth acknowledge Thee."

Many of the psalms have this motive exclusively and praise God "because He is good and His mercy everlasting." See for example Psalm 103 (Saturday at Lauds): "O Lord, my God, Thou art exceeding great. Thou hast put on praise and beauty, and art clothed with light as with a garment." In this psalm the human voice blends with all creation to adore and praise the Creator. It is praise carried to the point of enthusiasm.

There is in fact one Hour of the Office which is given over altogether to this motive of praise and is therefore called Lauds. It is the hour of dawn, of the rising sun, the hour of the resurrection of Christ, the sun of our spiritual life, and accordingly it chants the psalms of happiness and sings hymns of luminous joy to Christ:

"Of the Father effulgence bright,
Out of light evolving light,
Light from light, unfailing ray,
Day creative of the day.

Truest sun, upon us stream,
With Thy calm perpetual beam,
In the Spirit's still sunshine,
Making sense and thought divine."
(Monday at Lauds.)

"All ye works of the Lord, bless the Lord; ye angels of God, bless the Lord, ye sun and moon, ye showers and dew, ye fire and heat, ye ice and snow, ye mountains and ye beasts, ye sons of men, ye priests of the Lord, ye spirits and souls of the just ones, bless ye the Lord." (The canticle, *Benedicite*, Sunday at Lauds.)

b) *Prayer of thanksgiving*:

The motive of praise and adoration is often joined with that of thanksgiving. There are many splendid examples of this motive in the psalms, such as Psalm 117 (Sunday at Prime): "O praise the Lord, for He is good, for His mercy endureth forever. Let Israel now say that He is good, that His mercy endureth forever. Let them that fear the Lord now say, that His mercy endureth forever. In my trouble I called upon the Lord, and the Lord heard me and enlarged me. I shall not die but live, and shall declare the works of the Lord." This psalm is one of thanksgiving throughout.

Other examples of thanksgiving chants are the *Benedictus* at Lauds and the *Magnificat* at Vespers:

"Blessed be the Lord God of Israel, because He hath visited and wrought the redemption of His people."

"My soul doth magnify the Lord; and my spirit hath rejoiced in God my Savior. For He hath regarded the humility of His handmaid. He hath showed might with His arm. He hath exalted the humble. He hath filled the hungry with good things."

c) *Prayer of propitiation*:

The Breviary must necessarily give expression to the sense of our feebleness and nothingness. In doing so it covers a wide range, from the simple affirmation of our weakness as creatures to the deep cry of grief over our sins and from the abyss of dejection into which they have plunged us.

Recitation of the seven Penitential Psalms is hardly a common custom now as it was in former times, although these psalms are still to be found in some of our modern prayer-books. The *De Profundis* and the *Miserere* are still in frequent use, although many of us seem to think that they are to be referred exclusively to the dead. How many confessors today would venture to assign as a penance in confession the recitation of Psalm 68: "Save me, O God, for the waters are come in even unto my soul. I stick fast in the mire of the deep, and there is no sure standing. I am come into the depth of the sea, and a tempest hath overwhelmed me."

Or again, Psalm 21: "O God, my God, look upon me; why hast Thou forsaken me? Far from my salvation are the words of my sins. I am a worm and no man, the reproach of men and the outcast of the people."

And yet, what better way of expressing our repentance than by uniting our sorrow at having sinned with the sorrow of Christ as He weeps under the burden of our sins?

If we recite Compline daily we express our sorrow for sin when we repeat the *Confiteor*, a beautiful act of contrition.

d) *Prayer of impetration*:

Even those whose chief motive in prayer is self-interest will find their desires expressed in the Breviary, provided they do not limit themselves to petition for temporal things. In many of the psalms we are urged to ask for victory over the enemies of our salvation. The hymns do not forget to plead for both our bodily and spiritual needs. At the beginning of each Hour there is a formula of supplication: "Incline unto mine aid, O God; O Lord, make haste to help me." In the Office of a saint's day, when we praise God and thank Him on account of the glory rendered to Him by the life and merits of one of the apostles, or martyrs, or confessors, or virgins, we also ask that by His grace we may imitate the virtues and be helped by the example of the saint whose memory we celebrate. And finally, each mystery of the liturgical year includes a request for the particular grace which the collect of the day usually expresses.

2. The Breviary includes our chief customary prayers, such as morning and evening prayers and prayers of thanksgiving after Communion.

a) *Morning prayer*:

The morning prayer of the Breviary is the beautiful Hour of Prime. Besides the Our Father and Hail Mary and the Creed, which people generally recite in their morning prayer, Prime includes prayers which ask explicitly for God's help in view of the day that lies ahead, and this surely is an essential element in a morning prayer.

This Hour begins with the formula: "Incline unto mine aid, O God," a phrase especially appropriate at the beginning of the day. Then follows the beautiful hymn: *"Jam lucis orto sidere"*:

> "The star of morn to night succeeds;
> We therefore meekly pray,
> May God in all our words and deeds,
> Keep us from harm this day.
>
> May He in love restrain us still
> From tones of strife and words of ill
> And wrap around and close our eyes
> To earth's absorbing vanities.
>
> So when the weary day is o'er,
> And night and stillness come once more,
> Blameless and clean from spot of earth,
> We may repeat with reverent mirth:
>
> To God the Father glory be,
> And to His only Son,
> And to the Spirit, One in Three,
> While endless ages run. Amen."

Toward the end of Prime comes the prayer: "O Lord, God almighty, who has brought us to the beginning of this day, defend us in the same by Thy power, that we may not fall this day into any sin, but that all our thoughts, words and works may be directed to the fulfilment of Thy glory."

And again: "O Lord God, king of heaven and earth, vouchsafe this day to direct and sanctify, to rule and govern our hearts and bodies, our thoughts, words and deeds, in Thy law and in the works of Thy commandments, that now and ever we may, by Thy help, attain salvation and freedom, O Savior of the world, who livest and reignest for ever and ever, Amen."

There is also, before the short lesson of Prime, the prayer: "May the almighty God order our days and actions in His peace."

b) *Evening prayer*:

What a wonderful evening prayer the Breviary offers us in the Hour of Compline. It is distinctly the *"oratio ad decumbendum,"* the prayer before retiring to rest, or as we say ordinarily, night prayer.

It begins straightway: "May the Lord almighty grant us a quiet night and a perfect end." Then follows a warning against temptation: "Brethren, be sober and watch. For your adversary, the devil, goeth about as a roaring lion, seeking whom he may devour; whom resist ye, strong in faith."

Next comes the *Confiteor* and an absolution for the night. And then the psalmody, in three psalms chosen to inspire confidence and peace at the end of a day that may have been wearisome and before the night's repose. After these comes the beautiful hymn of nightfall:

> "Now with the fast-departing light,
> Maker of all, we ask of Thee,
> Of Thy great mercy, through the night,
> Our guardian and defense to be.
>
> Far off let idle visions fly;
> No phantom of the night molest.
> Curb Thou our raging enemy,
> That we in chaste repose may rest."

The supernatural confidence which is voiced all throughout Compline has its reason in the divine gift of sanctifying grace by which we are made children of God in baptism and in which we live. The Church reminds us of this each evening, bidding us, as it were by a delicate allusion, to thank God for the great grace of our baptism: "But Thou, O Lord, art in us, and Thy holy name is invoked upon us; forsake us not, O Lord our God."

And so we are able to say with full confidence: "Into Thy hands, O Lord, I commend my spirit; for Thou hast redeemed us, O God of truth."

Likewise delicate as the allusion to our baptism is the reference to our death in the words: "Now dost Thou dismiss Thy servant, O Lord, according to Thy word in peace." Sleep is an image of death, and it is right that we be mindful of that final hour in the spirit of Simeon when he held the Christ-child in his arms.

Moreover, death is to be regarded as a reawakening in Christ and to everlasting life. Therefore we pray: "Save us, O Lord, while we are awake, and guard us when we sleep, that we may watch with Christ and rest in peace."

This beautiful night prayer, Compline, ends as it began, once more asking God's blessing upon the house and all who dwell therein: "Visit, we beseech Thee, O Lord, this house and family, and drive far from it all snares of the enemy; let Thy holy angels dwell therein, who may keep us in peace, and let Thy blessing be always upon us."

c) *Thanksgiving after Communion*:

There are many prayers in the Breviary which may be used for this purpose. Not to speak of the various psalms, like Psalm 83: "How lovely are Thy tabernacles, O Lord of hosts," or Psalm 22: "The Lord ruleth me, and I shall want nothing," which tells of the joy of being sheltered and cared for by divine mercy and satisfied in spiritual hunger and thirst, one may find an abundant supply of prayers after Communion in the Office of the Blessed Sacrament, for example the antiphons like: "O sacred banquet" (Second Vespers), or the hymns like the *Pange lingua* (First Vespers). These will foster piety more effectively than will the sentimental and exaggerated prayers of some of our prayer books which easily become insipid on account of their lack of sound doctrinal substance.

3. The Breviary contains material suitable for particular devotions.

a) *Devotion to the Holy Trinity*:

It is unnecessary to insist at any length that the Breviary fosters this devotion. The very recitation itself, the whole orientation of the Breviary, the ever-recurring doxologies, constantly direct us to the Holy Trinity. This is so evident that it needs no emphasis.

b) *Devotion to the Blessed Sacrament*:

In addition to what has been said regarding prayers after Communion, what a mine of eucharistic devotion is the Office for Thursday in Holy Week and that for the feast of Corpus Christi with its entire octave. The psalms, antiphons and hymns are an inexhaustible source of eucharistic prayer. The lessons from St. Paul, St. Augustine, St. John Chrysostom and St. Thomas are passages which for their elevated thought and fervent language rank among the masterpieces of Christian literature. We are at the very sources here, from which all other manuals of devotion have drawn their best content on this subject.

c) *Devotion to the Passion of our Lord*:

There are many passages in the Breviary which foster this devotion, so dear to fervent souls. Many of the saints have found their delight in the messianic psalms relating to the Passion, such as Psalm 21: "O God, my God, look upon me; why hast Thou forsaken me?"

The former editions of the Breviary contained special Offices relating to the Passion and assigned to the Fridays of Lent which are still serviceable in private devotion. The present Office during Passiontide and Holy Week, especially that of Good Friday, offer abundant material. How much more vivid is the experience of these days of Holy Week when along with the services contained in the Missal one follows the Office of *Tenebrae!*

d) *Devotion to the Sacred Heart:*

The new Office for the feast and octave of the Sacred Heart is a complete manual of this devotion. Why not give preference to these prayers which are offered to our divine Lord in the united prayer of the entire Church?

e) *Devotion to the Blessed Virgin:*

What an abundance of prayer formulas does the Breviary offer in honor of our Lady! Besides the many feast days celebrating the various mysteries, joyful, sorrowful and glorious, with hymns, lessons, antiphons, one more beautiful than another, there are the daily invocations of the Queen of heaven in the *Salve Regina*, the *Alma Redemptoris Mater*, the *Ave Regina coelorum*, the *Regina coeli*, according to the season. The *Magnificat* occurs daily at Vespers. Here again, the Breviary is an inexhaustible source for this devotion.

f) *Devotion to the Saints:*

There are many saints' days throughout the year, for each of which the Church has arranged a series of prayers in the divine Office. If then we wish to honor such or such saint, why not use these Breviary prayers composed by the Church, in preference to others composed by private persons. To take the case of St. Teresa of Lisieux for example, why should popular devotion neglect the concise liturgical formulas and prefer the interminable litanies and similar prayers of private origin? Are the latter considered to be more efficacious on account of their length? It is true, however, that some of these private prayers have indulgences attached to them and deserve respect for that reason.

g) *Devotion to the Souls in Purgatory*:

It is a well-known fact that the Breviary contains excellent prayers for the dead, and layfolk have ample opportunity to be acquainted with the Requiem Mass and Office. Yet it seems that not many of them are prompted by devotion to the dead to assist at Vespers or Lauds of the Requiem Office, the latter of which, by the way, is often chanted on the preceding evening, so that the funeral service may not be too long.[1]

4. The Breviary contains prayers appropriate to all our particular intentions and corresponding to our personal sentiments.

a) *Intentions*:

For the Church: *e.g.*, "May Thy constant mercy, O Lord, cleanse and fortify Thy Church, and since without Thee she cannot abide in safety, ever govern her by Thy grace" (Fifteenth Sunday after Pentecost).

For one's own family: *e.g.*, "Visit, we beseech Thee, O Lord, this house and family, and drive far from it all snares of the enemy; let Thy holy angels dwell therein who may keep us in peace, and let Thy blessing be always upon us" (daily at Compline).

And: "Look down, O Lord, we beseech Thee, on this Thy family, for which our Lord Jesus Christ did not hesi-

[1] The author refers here to European custom. In the United States the laity are less well acquainted with the Office of the Dead.

tate to be delivered into the hands of sinners and to suffer the torments of the cross" (Holy Week).

For growth in Christian perfection: *e.g.*, "O God of hosts, the giver of all good things, implant in our hearts the love of Thy name; make us to grow in fervor, foster in us that which is good; and in Thy loving kindness of that which Thou fosterest be Thou also the safeguard" (Sixth Sunday after Pentecost).

For sinners: *e.g.*, see the collects in the Missal and the corresponding orations in the Offices of the season of Lent and those of Requiem.

We might go on in this way to point out examples of prayers for all possible intentions.

b) *Personal sentiments*:

In the same way we might point out in the Breviary examples showing the expression of the most varied sentiments. Thus:

Joy: Psalm 102: "Bless the Lord, O my soul, and all that is within me, bless His holy name" (Saturday at Compline). And Psalm 22: "The Lord ruleth me, I shall want nothing" (Thursday at Prime). And Psalm 132: "Behold how good and how pleasant it is for brethren to dwell together in unity" (Thursday as Vespers).

Confidence: The response at Compline: "Into Thy hands, O Lord, I commend my spirit," and the majority of the psalms of Compline.

Hope: Psalm 192, the *De Profundis* is a beautiful act of hope.

Repentance: Psalm 50, the *Miserere*; and the seven Penitential Psalms.

Trial and suffering: Many of the psalms sound the very depths of these emotions. So also do the collects, like that of the Fourth Sunday after Epiphany: "O God, who knowest that we are beset by perils greater than our human weakness may withstand; grant us health of soul and body that what we suffer for our sins we may overcome by Thy help."

From these various examples we may certainly conclude that the Breviary, along with the Missal, is the best of prayer books for all the faithful.

PART TWO

THE BREVIARY AS A MANUAL OF DISCURSIVE PRAYER OR MEDITATION

As in the preceding part, on vocal prayer, we shall begin by stating a number of objections which are usually offered to the suggestion that the Breviary be used as a manual of mental prayer.

I. Objections:

1. I already have a method of meditation which satisfies me. I could not possibly meditate otherwise. And the Breviary method is altogether different.

2. Unless one is already well advanced in the practice of meditation, one will surely become confused in trying to meditate from the Breviary. Its topics are not clearly arranged. There are no preludes and the matter is not divided into points. Hence, while I admire the idea, I do not think it is practical in my case.

3. The Breviary is indeed very beautiful as a liturgical and collective prayer. It is the official prayer of the Church. But in my personal relations with God I need something less official and less theological, something that appeals more to the heart.

II. The question in the light of history:

Are we advocating something novel? One does well to be mistrustful of novelties. Let us see if this idea of using the Breviary as a manual of private meditation has never been thought of until now.

a) *In the first Christian centuries*:

We have already spoken of the ancient Vigil service in dealing with vocal prayer. It did not consist entirely of vocal, *i.e.*, recited or chanted prayer. There were also spaces of silence during which the worshipers meditated, reflecting on what had been said and heard. This assimilation of the doctrine of the inspired Scriptures was a preparation for the eucharistic Sacrifice at dawn and for the receiving of the Lord in eucharistic Communion. This method of meditation continued throughout the period of the persecutions, and we read in the Acts of the Martyrs that in their prisons they engaged "alternately in the chant of hymns and in silent meditation."

The continents and virgins of this period, corresponding to the later religious communities, were especially devoted to this ideal of union with the divine Word by meditation upon the inspired word of the Scriptures. It supplemented the transitory union which they experienced in the Holy Eucharist. Meditation on the Gospels and the frequent repetition of the psalms gave real continuity to their prayer-life. "*Oportet semper orare*—we ought always to pray." It was this desire for continual contact with Christ that prompted St. Cecelia to carry about with her always the text of the Gospels.

b) *From the fourth to the sixth centuries*:

This period produced an abundance of homilies and commentaries, explanations given at the liturgical services of the Scriptural texts that had been read there. And what are these but meditations on the material contained in the public prayer of the Church? The faithful took these meditations to heart and in that way carried them home, somewhat as in the previous period of the persecutions the early Christians were allowed to take the Holy Eucharist to their homes.

When St. Ambrose says that daybreak should always find a virgin with the psalter in her hands, he means that it should be her manual of meditation in the earlier hours.

c) *From the sixth century onwards*:

Monasticism regarded the text of the divine Office as the best of material for meditation. St. Benedict's phrase: "*Mens concordet voci*—let the mind accord with the voice" means that what is recited or chanted in the Office should furnish food for thought and that mind and voice should go hand in hand. Vocal prayer and meditation were so intimately united in the divine Office that St. Benedict did not regard them as two things apart, nor did he in his Rule appoint a special time for meditation. He allowed his monks to pause after the vocal recitation and to let the prayer find its echo in the soul.[1] In other instances of monastic rule the custom was to recite the psalms very slowly, with long pauses, so that the mind might follow from verse to verse at equal pace with the words of uttered praise.

d) *In the Middle Ages*:

During this period prayer-life became very intense. There appear schools of contemplative life in which systematic prayer is cultivated alongside the official prayer of the liturgy. The distinction between vocal and mental

[1] See the excellent paper presented by Dom I. Ryelandt at the Liturgical Week at Maredsous in 1912: *Breviaire et Meditation. Cours et Conf. des Semaines Liturgiques*, 1913, pp. 170-187.

prayer is sharpened. The homilies of an Augustine and the sermons of a Bernard, formed from the material of the Office, and in their own minds springing from it, are now made material for prayer apart from the Office.

Thus in time there appear interminable divisions and headings devised in order to guide the soul through the mass of pious considerations which authors drew from a text. The meditations of Ludolph of Saxony on the Gospel text are a typical example of this procedure which by his time had been followed for many years.

Meditation according to "points" had thus become quite the fashion in the fifteenth century, and we find it recommended by reputable authors like Mauburnus.[1]

e) *In the sixteenth century:*

The classicism of this period, with its taste for methodical procedure, tends to discourage meditation upon any texts that are not arranged systematically.

Moreover, in the Renaissance period people seem to have less time for prayer, although on the other hand there is an increasing supply of material.

Consequently there is a demand for methodical meditation books which writers hasten to supply. And so we observe the appearance of "books of exercises" (*ejercitatorios*) which provide a system of training to render the soul ready and apt in prayer.

Another characteristic of this period, which also contributed to divert attention from liturgical prayer, was the disposition to distinguish the faculties of the soul as the body was dissected in anatomy. It was a period of intro-

[1] *Meditatorium*, m. 3.

spection when it became the fashion in meditation to take the soul apart piece by piece.

St. Francis de Sales, while he recommends methodical prayer, still advocates great liberty in method. St. Teresa refuses to be bound by rigid rules and draws her inspiration directly from the divine Office. But St. Ignatius, following the procedure of Cisneros, confines the soul within the method of his *Spiritual Exercises*, which indeed offer a marvelous system of training but at the same time allow prayer-life to proceed quite apart from the vocal and public prayer of the Church.

f) *In the seventeenth and eighteenth centuries*:

Methodical prayer apart from the divine Office receives a new emphasis in the Sulpician method.

As conceived by Cardinal de Berulle, M. de Condren, and M. Olier, who reduced the method to rule, it still allows considerable liberty and shows a resemblance to the methods of St. Francis de Sales and St. Teresa, with a tendency to stress the affective element. But M. Tronson made it an austere process of reflections and petitions. Devised for seminarians, this method was now applied in the novitiates and seminaries of the nineteenth century with a strictness that made meditation an ascetical exercise pure and simple. And so it found its place in seminary regulations on equal footing with the recitation of the Rosary and the Way of the Cross.

Thus in short we have quite turned aside from the Church's original conception of prayer as being a vocal and official prayer animated and assimilated by the activity of the soul.

III. Reply to objections:

1. *I have a method which satisfies me*:

We certainly do not wish to depreciate any of the accepted methods. They do mark progress in the sense that they afford spiritual training and render the soul more apt to grasp the material of prayer. And where life is standardized as it is today, they fill a need and facilitate intensive work with economy of time.

However, a method becomes harmful if it enslaves. Suarez, in speaking of methods of prayer, says: "These aids are not intended to imprison the soul nor to present a barrier to the Holy Spirit who must be free to move His creature as He wills. They simply show us how to set to work in cases where the Holy Spirit does not incite us by a special grace, and, once such grace is given, they render us prompt to receive it and to feel and follow it."[1]

Finally, a method is one thing and a manual of meditation is another. Without departing from one's favorite method, one may with advantage substitute the Breviary in place of the accustomed manual, at least now and then. The manuals produced since the sixteenth century, in conformity with the modern methods of prayer, are open to this objection that they are inclined to neglect the rich dogmatic sources of the Church's prayer (the psalms, hymns, lessons and orations of the Missal and Breviary) and to lay stress beyond due proportion upon the examination of virtues and similar introspections.

2. *The Breviary is for advanced persons*:

You need not be more advanced than were the simple monks of the sixth century who had no other prayer books. Moreover, we are not insisting that you must mas-

[1] *De religione Soc. Jesu*, I, IX, C. VI, 3.

ter the entire Breviary, but that you avail yourself of some of the material which it offers. There are so many manuals. Why does not someone prepare a manual based on the psalms or the lessons or other parts of the Breviary? And if so desired the matter can be arranged in "points" and provided with preludes and resolutions. In fact we already have meditation books on the psalms and hymns of the Breviary.

But even apart from such ready-made manuals, one would be quite mistaken to imagine that there are no "points" in the Breviary itself or that it is impossible to make a methodical meditation from the Breviary alone. There are Offices, as we shall show by examples, in which the three nocturns, or again the three lessons of a nocturn, are so many points relating to the saint or mystery of the day and furnishing material quite complete and easily grasped by beginners.

3. *The Breviary does not appeal to the heart*:

What a mistake it is to conceive the official, collective, liturgical prayer of the Church and one's private converse with God as two very distinct kinds of prayer. With this misunderstanding liturgical prayer becomes mere formal ceremony from which all intimate feeling is supposed to be excluded. If liturgical prayer does not appeal to your heart, it is because you do not put your heart into it and because in your case liturgical prayer lacks the accord of voice and soul. One is inclined to smile on hearing it said that the psalms, or the lessons from St. Ambrose or St. Bernard or St. Bonaventure, or the hymns "do not appeal to the heart." Those who say this may well consider if it is not rather their own meditation that is studied and formal and lacking in affection.

IV. Positive advantages:

It is evident enough that the foregoing objections are founded on sentiment rather than on reason. Nor are they able to hold their ground in view of the solid advantages which the Breviary affords as a manual of meditation. We have not the least intention to discourage the use of other manuals which at certain times especially may be very helpful, but we maintain that objectively considered the Breviary offers the greater guarantee of authority and sincerity and a richer variety of material. What, then, are its chief advantages?

1. *Breviary meditation places us in close contact with our High-priest, Christ Jesus, as teacher.*

Our Lord and High-priest feeds us with His body and blood in the Mass and with His words in the Office: "*Panis vitae et intellectus*—the bread of life and of understanding." The words of the Office are not only words of praise. In His priestly office, Christ is turned both toward God and toward man; toward God His Father in praise of Him, toward man for our instruction. The Church, the mystical body of Christ, intimately united with Him, is likewise turned toward God and toward man in the double function of praise and instruction. The words of the divine Office at one and the same time serve this twofold purpose. Meditation enables us to understand them. The profound meaning of these words upon our lips thus penetrates our mind and heart. Meditation on the orations, the hymns, the psalms, the lessons from the Old and New Testaments, puts us in direct and intimate contact with this teaching authority. It is Christ Himself who enters within us while in private meditation on these texts we are one in spirit with the chant of the Church.

2. The Breviary brings us to the authentic sources of true piety.

True piety is that which prompts us to greater zest in worship and consequently to greater zeal in the service of God. The chief sources of such piety are:

a) *Sacred Scripture*:

The content of the Breviary is derived chiefly from the Bible, so that to meditate upon the Breviary is for the most part to meditate upon the inspired word of the sacred Scriptures. "I have been delighted in the way of Thy testimonies," says the psalmist, "I will not forget Thy words" (Psalm 118). The reproach voiced by Protestants, that Catholics do not read the Bible, certainly does not apply to those who use the Breviary as their manual of meditation.

b) *Tradition*:

How many are there today who still meditate upon the writings of the Fathers of the Church? In the lessons and homilies of the Breviary we may follow the thought of these great teachers, listening to St. Leo, St. Augustine, St. Ambrose, St. Gregory, while they instruct us in virtue in conformity with the mystery of the day. Read, for example, on Christmas or Easter or the feast of the Seven Sorrows of Mary, the commentaries of St. Leo, St. Gregory and St. Bernard.

In meditating upon these texts we need have no fear of going astray from the right paths of true piety. There is no danger here of illusions and of spiritual aberrations as there is in certain manuals which stir up our sensibilities by appeals to the imagination and which neglect to furnish the sound doctrinal foundation without which emotion is exercised to no avail. The Fathers of the Church are the authentic interpreters of Catholic doctrine, and meditation based on their writings will enlarge our spiritual horizon.

3. *The Breviary is the Church's own composition and unites us with the mind of the Church.*

"*Semper in psalmis meditemur*—let us always meditate on the psalms," says the Church in the Matins hymn on the Sundays after Pentecost.

Meditation on the Breviary keeps us in constant union with the mind of the Church as we proceed day by day through the cycle of the liturgical year. There are those who may perhaps be meditating on the passion of our Lord during the Christmas octave because they happen to be at that place in their manual; or who are concerned in their private meditation with the study and practice of some virtue without any regard to the fact that they may be at the time within the octave of Easter or of Corpus Christi. This certainly is not the most logical way.

Moreover, it involves a certain danger of harm to the sincerity of our mental prayer. The critical spirit, the desire for what is real and genuine, are characteristic of our modern mentality. We have a strong dislike for the mere conventional and the artificial and we instinctively avoid these in literature and in the arts and in science. Thus there is also a disposition to give up the practice of meditation because there seems to be something artificial about it.

Certainly with most people the over-systematized methods of private meditation are more likely to grow monotonous than the broader and freer method, which consists in simply adapting oneself to the liturgical life of the Church. In the latter case we may feel quite sure about the value of a procedure which has stood the test of centuries.

In meditating on the Breviary texts, one feels that one does not act alone and simply on one's own resources. There is the consciousness of union in mind as well as in word with the larger life of the Church, of intimate union in the mystical body of Christ.

4. *The Breviary offers a greater wealth of material than do the other manuals.*

The systematic manuals always represent more or less the personality of their author, and may not therefore correspond well with our own tastes or with the period in which we live. A manual of this kind has its relatively narrow limitations.

The Breviary represents the slow growth of the liturgical tradition throughout centuries. Each successive period has brought its contribution to enrich by its reflections the ancient store of the holy Scriptures and the primitive Mysteries. There is material here to satisfy every taste. According to one's particular temperament or aptitude, one may dwell upon the entire theme of a given Office or upon any portion of its text. There is splendid material in all the various elements of which the Office is composed, the orations, the hymns, lessons, and psalms. One single oration alone may furnish material for a lengthy meditation; some of the hymns are full of magnificent ideas; the psalms and lessons contain a great wealth of doctrinal material. We hope to make this plain by means of the examples which we shall adduce.

V. Practical applications:

Before describing the method of Breviary meditation, let us first observe what elements are to be found in all methods, and are therefore the essential ones. We shall find that Breviary meditation includes all of them.

Dom Ryelandt, in agreement with all the approved authors, whether ancient or modern, gives us the following definition: "Meditation means reflection—in the presence of God—on the truths of salvation—calculated to convince the mind with a view to better action."

On the basis of this definition, we may observe that all methods of meditation insist upon three objectives:

I. The preliminary disposition of the soul.

II. The assimilation of the material.

III. The determination of the mental and moral resultants.

These three objectives are subdivided under various headings in the various methods:

I. *The preliminary disposition of the soul*:

1) Attention to the presence of God (in all the methods).
2) Disposition of the faculties of the soul:
    a) "Invocations" (Salesian and Sulpician methods).
    b) "Statement of the mystery" (Salesian); "Prelude" (Ignatian); "Composition of place" (various methods); etc.

These processes are intended to rightly dispose the sense faculties and the imagination, so that being properly engaged they will not disturb the intellect in its recollection and in its examination of the meditation topic.

II. *The assimilation of the material*:

Nearly all the methods begin here with a division of the subject into its "points" (Ignatian and Sulpician) or "considerations" (Salesian). The memory, intellect and will are engaged in their proper tasks ("exercises" in the Ignatian method; "adoration, communion and cooperation" in the Sulpician method). The ancient methods were less analytic and advised a continual "rumination" or revision of the text (Cassian).

III. *The determination of the resultants:*

All the methods are concerned to reach definite conclusions. These usually come at the end of the meditation, but may also occur during its course in the "exercise of the will" (Ignatian) or the "cooperation" (Sulpician).

Having noted these essential features of all meditation methods, as we turn now to the Breviary, let us consider it, as a manual of meditation, from two points of view:

1. The Breviary as a book which offers a great variety of beautiful topics for meditation.

2. The Breviary as itself a manual of meditation with a method of its own.

1. THE BREVIARY IS A VERITABLE MINE OF BEAUTIFUL MEDITATION TOPICS.

What a wonderful meditation book is the psalter! And many of the psalms will be found divisible into "points."[1] Let us take for example Psalm 109:

FIRST POINT: The kingship of the Messiah: a) His throne (v. 1); b) His scepter (v. 2); c) His authority (v. 3).

SECOND POINT: The priesthood of the Messiah: a) in the offering of sacrifice (v. 4); b) in judgment (v. 6).

With the topic thus arranged one may proceed to apply one's favorite method in the preliminary disposition of soul, in the assimilation of the subject and in the determination of the results.

---

[1] We do not mean to suggest that meditation must necessarily be according to "points"; our intention is here to show that those who prefer that method need not hesitate to use the Breviary as their manual. See the objection above.

The lessons of the Breviary also furnish a whole series of topics. Take for example one of the lessons of the second nocturn, a homily of St. Fulgentius, for the feast of St. Stephen:

FIRST POINT: the martyrdom of St. Stephen considered in relation to the feast of Christmas.

SECOND POINT: the contrast between our Lord who assumes our flesh in coming down for our redemption, and St. Stephen who lays aside his body to ascend into heaven.

THIRD POINT: the charity of St. Stephen who prays for his executioners.

Here we have the three points of a well-arranged meditation. And those who have their heart set on the Ignatian or Sulpician methods will find no difficulty in adding the "composition of place" and a "spiritual bouquet" in reference to the virtue of love toward God and neighbor.

In a similar way one may observe the preliminary rules of one's accustomed method and then proceed to meditate upon the beautiful sermon of St. Bernard which the Breviary offers us on the feast of the Holy Name.

The second nocturn lessons on a saint's day are in fact a summary biography which the Church proposes for our meditation.

The homily on the Gospel of the day presented in the third nocturn may easily serve in like manner as the topic of a meditation according to one's accustomed rule. Take for example the penetrating homily of St. Gregory for the feast of St. Andrew in which this great teacher explains that the merit of our renunciation is not to be measured by the value of the thing renounced but by the degree of our inward control of the very desire of possession.

We could go on thus in our search for material and find another series of topics—this time for those who are not bound by methods and who take what is good wherever they find it—in the marvelous orations of the Breviary. Many of these orations which appear quite simple contain in highly condensed form a whole world of ideas.

Let our example here be the oration for the Fourth Sunday after Epiphany. It suggests first of all the subject of "our human frailty." Next, this sense of humility is intensified by the consideration of "the many perils that surround us." And then, from God "who knows these things" we ask "strength of soul and body" to the supernatural end that we may "overcome" these evils. We ask for fortitude that we may "repel by God's grace those evils which are avoidable and that we may endure with courage those that are the penalties consequent upon our sins." In a meditation of this kind all our faculties are engaged, the senses and imagination, the intellect and will.

We need not go on multiplying examples. The wonder is that with all our manuals of meditation composed by pious authors, there are so few based exclusively on passages from the Breviary or the Missal, on the psalms, Scripture readings, hymns, orations, homilies and biographies of the saints.[1]

2. THE BREVIARY CONSIDERED AS ITSELF A MANUAL OF MEDITATION WITH A METHOD OF ITS OWN.

This proposition will probably not be conceded as readily as the preceding one. Let us examine it. We have in mind especially the Matins Hour. One must remember that Matins had its origin in the nightly Vigil in the

---

[1] Mention should be made of the *Meditations Liturgiques* of Dom Gaspar Lefebvre as an excellent example; and also of books of meditation on the psalms, such as: *Psaumes et cantiques du Breviaire Romain*, by Pere Hugueny.

ancient epoch. In the Vigil service the early Christians spent the night in meditation upon the particular mystery which was to be the theme of the Eucharist service at dawn. Thus down to the present time the Matins Hour should be understood as an abbreviation of the ancient Vigil, a well-ordered meditation by which the Church prepares us for the holy sacrifice of the Mass. It is the Church's wish that a priest shall have recited Matins before he approaches the altar to celebrate Mass.

The method of the Church is less rigid and regimented than are the modern ones. Yet it is well-ordered and contains all the essential elements which we have already named. We now proceed to prove this.

A. THE MATINS HOUR CONTAINS THE ESSENTIAL ELEMENTS WHICH ALL THE METHODS HAVE IN COMMON.

I. *The preliminary disposition of the soul*:

a) Attention to the presence of God:

What else is the invitatory antiphon and psalm? Does not the Church intend precisely to invite us to place our soul in the divine presence when at the beginning of the Office we read: "The Lord is our maker; O come, let us adore Him"; "Unto the eternal King all live; O come, let us adore Him"; "The Lord, He is the King of apostles: O come, let us adore Him"; "Unto us the Christ is born; O come, let us adore Him"; etc.

b) Disposition of faculties:

This is accomplished by means of invocative phrases and announcements of the mystery of the day. What prelude can surpass the hymn which follows the invitatory, in which the Church proposes the mystery which is the central theme of a given day and which is adorned in the hymn with images and emotions in invocative form'

II. *The body of the meditation*:

The lessons of Matins constitute the chief substance or body of the meditation. In many cases the three nocturns are three principal "points" or aspects under which the Church presents a mystery for our meditation. And these in turn are subdivided into secondary considerations in the three lessons of each nocturn. The first nocturn generally presents the symbol or figure of the mystery drawn from the Old Testament. The second nocturn narrates the historical event or states the fact of the mystery. The third nocturn shows the moral application and supplies the motive which is intended to influence the will and to direct it in the formulation of its resolutions.

If the Office of a given day does not celebrate some mystery of our Lord or of the Virgin Mother but rather the feast of a saint, the first nocturn lessons from the Common apply to the saint some passage from the Scriptures.

III. *Determination of the resultants*:

The homily of the third nocturn usually contains some moral lesson, and it remains for us to apply this personally in our resolutions. We will find this application suggested in the oration of the day, which may also serve as a "spiritual bouquet" or "thought for the day."

B. THE BREVIARY METHOD OF MEDITATION WHICH WE HAVE THUS INDICATED WILL APPEAR MORE PLAINLY IF WE CONSIDER A FEW EXAMPLES.

First Example: The Office of the Exaltation of the Cross (September 14).

I. *Disposition of soul*:

1) Attention to the presence of God (**and here of** Christ on the cross). The invitatory antiphon: "Christ,

our King, uplifted for us on the cross; O come, let us adore Him"; and the psalm, "Venite."

2) Disposition of faculties:

a) Invocation: the hymn:

> "Sing, my tongue the glorious battle
> With completed victory rife,
> And above the cross' trophy
> Tell the triumph of the strife;
> How the world's Redeemer conquered
> By surrendering of His life."

and the final doxology: "To the Trinity be glory."

b) Preludes, or proposal of the mystery:

This goes on through the course of the hymn. One need not linger over every one of the stanzas, but may pause here or there according to one's disposition at the moment. For example:

> "Noted then this wood, the ruin
> Of the ancient wood to quell";

> "The royal banners forward go;
> The cross shines forth in mystic glow"

> "O tree of beauty, tree of light,
> O tree with royal purple dight"
>   (Vespers hymn).

> "Faithful cross, above all other,
> One and only noble tree

> "Sweetest wood and sweetest iron,
> Sweetest weight is hung on thee"
>   (Lauds hymn).

The beautiful antiphons of this Office may also be used to serve as preludes.

II. *The body of the meditation*:

FIRST POINT: first nocturn: lessons from the Book of Numbers: the story of the brazen serpent (a figure of our Lord uplifted on the cross), the instrument of salvation for the Hebrew people, disheartened and bitten by the serpents, in their distress in the desert.

SECOND POINT: second nocturn: the historical episode: the recovery of the true cross from Chosroes, king of Persia, by the emperor Heraclius, and the ceremony of its exaltation.

THIRD POINT: third nocturn: a splendid homily of St. Leo which stirs the emotions and prompts the will to an effective love of Christ's cross, and which concludes with the beautiful thought of the Mass as the climax of all sacrifice and the sacrament of Christian unity.

III. *Determination of resultants*:

There are many resolutions to choose from when the material is so rich: a better understanding of Christ's cross and of the holy sacrifice of the Mass; gratitude toward our divine Savior; a sense of joy in His victory; the willing acceptance of our daily sufferings. The oration of the day, repeated several times and taken well to heart, will fix these sentiments in a concise and concrete formula. We are "gladdened year by year in the recurrence of this feast of the exaltation of the holy cross," and we ask that we may "understand here in our life on earth the mystery of our redemption" and that as we live according to the mystery of the cross in the daily sacrifice of the Mass and in the daily following of our Lord, so may we "merit the heavenly reward that He has promised us."

If we thus make the Matins Hour our Vigil of the Mass, how fruitful will be our participation in the holy Sacrifice as we follow its course with the Missal in hand and in union with the priest at the altar.

Second Example: The Office of the Seven Sorrows of the Blessed Virgin (September 15); a meditation of more affective character.

I. *Disposition of soul:*

1) Attention to the presence of Mary and of her divine Son and of the Holy Trinity. The invitatory antiphon: "Let us take our stand by the cross, in company with Mary, the Mother of Jesus; a sword of sorrow hath pierced her soul."

2) Disposition of faculties:

Invocations and preludes or proposal of the mystery in the hymn:

> "Come, darkness, spread o'er heaven thy pall
> And hide, O sun, thy face,
> While we that bitter death recall,
> With all its dire disgrace."

> "And thou with tearful cheek wast there,
> But with a heart of steel."

> "Yet still erect in majesty
> Thou didst the sight sustain;
> O more than martyr, not to die
> Amid such cruel pain."

These are lines from the hymn of First Vespers. The antiphons throughout the Office may also serve as sympathetic preludes.

II. *The body of the meditation*:

FIRST POINT: first nocturn: the Old Testament figure or symbol, Jerusalem in ruin, abandoned and desolate, and lamented by Jeremiah.

SECOND POINT: second nocturn: the historical event, a mystical one, the interior martyrdom of Mary as told by St. Bernard in tender language.

THIRD POINT: third nocturn: the moral of the mystery as set forth in the homily of St. Ambrose. He tells us that the meaning of this mystic death at which we have assisted is that of an oblation, a voluntary oblation, an oblation for the redeeming of mankind, a bitter oblation made by Christ Himself, who gave His mother to mankind.

The responsories of this Office are told off like so many pearls in a sequence of sorrows; or they recall the old Greek drama in which the chorus appears at intervals to re-echo the tragic theme.

III. *Determination of resultants*:

Again, there are many resolutions offered for our choice; chiefly the loving and reverent thought of Mary's sorrow and the resolution to penetrate more deeply with her into the mystery of our Lords' passion. The oration of the day expresses this thought concisely. After reference to the sword of which Simeon spoke, we ask that "while we contemplate her sorrows we may obtain the saving fruit of Christ's passion." This prayer is repeated in the Office throughout the day.

Third Example: The feast of St. Bartholomew (August 24).

I. *Disposition of soul*:

a) Invitatory antiphon: "The Lord, the King of apostles; O come, let us adore Him."

b) Prelude: the hymn:

> "The Lord's eternal gifts,
> The apostles' mighty praise,
> Their victories and high reward,
> Sing we in joyful lays."

> "Lords of the churches they,
> Triumphant chiefs of war."

> "Theirs was the saint's high faith,
> And quenchless hope's pure glow,
> And perfect charity which laid
> The world's fell tyrant low."

> In them the Father shone,
> In them the Son o'ercame,
> In them the Holy Spirit wrought
> And filled their hearts with flame."

II. *The body of the meditation*:

FIRST POINT: first nocturn: lessons from the Common of Apostles. In the First Epistle to the Corinthians. St. Paul outlines the character of an apostle: one whose life and conduct are shaped by his faith and whose conscience is established in the law of God; one who is humble and willing to be humiliated; who when despised and persecuted for the sake of Christ abounds in joy; one who regards his converts as children whom he has begotten in the Lord.

SECOND POINT: second nocturn: the apostolic character as apparent in the life of St. Bartholomew; his missionary zeal and missionary activity in India and in Armenia; the conversion of the king Polymius and his queen, and of twelve cities; the jealousy of the pagan priests and the persecution of St. Bartholomew by Astyages, the brother of the king; and finally the horrible martyrdom.

THIRD POINT: third nocturn: a homily of St. Ambrose: the Gospel episode of the solitary prayer of Christ on the mountain during the night before His mission of the apostles, a prayer for all mankind expressive of His own mission and the share in it which He is about to entrust to His disciples.

The homily begins with the words: "All they who go up into the mountain are the great and the aspiring." St. Ambrose exhorts us to follow the Lord up the mountain as the apostles did by their great deeds, and to be assiduous in prayer. Moreover, he reminds us to pray for those who labor in the ministry, for the Lord chose feeble men so that the faith might triumph not by the force of natural talent but by the supernatural power of prayer.

III. *Determination of resultants*:

Joy in the glory of St. Bartholomew and in the victory of his martyrdom; devotion to the Church in which and for which he labored, and which we should know as the mystical Christ, Christ always dwelling among us and guiding us through His visible vicar and the successors of the apostles; interest in the missionary works of our own time, and prayer that these efforts may win ever greater numbers to the love of God.

The oration of the day will keep us mindful of such thoughts: "Almighty and everlasting God, who hast given us the solemn and holy joy of this day, the feast of Thy blessed apostle Bartholomew; grant unto Thy Church, we beseech Thee, both to love what he believed and to preach what he taught."

Thus we see that the Church has her own method of meditation, a method quite her own, which we certainly ought not to ignore. She has her own manual, the Breviary, a wonderful repertory of meditations which no other manual can surpass.

PART THREE

THE BREVIARY AS A MANUAL OF AFFECTIVE PRAYER

We distinguish affective prayer from discursive prayer or meditation, of which we spoke in the preceding part. In affective prayer the soul proceeds by movements of the heart rather than of the mind. Whereas in meditation or discursive prayer, the resolutions toward betterment of life are the product of reasoned thought, in affective prayer they spring from loving intuition. We may briefly define affective prayer in the words of Father Poulain as "that kind of mental prayer in which the affections are numerous or occupy more place than the considerations or arguments."[1]

This kind of prayer has many degrees of intensity, corresponding to the various affective experiences of the soul. However, we may distinguish two principal degrees:

1. Ordinary affective prayer, in which affective intuitions predominate but are still accompanied by various movements of the discursive intellect.

2. Prayer of simplicity, or of active recollection, in which affective intuition predominates without admixture of the discursive elements.

Affective prayer must also be distinguished from the still higher contemplative prayer (of which we shall speak

[1] Poulain, *The Graces of Interior Prayer*, p. 8.

later). For in contemplative prayer the intuition is produced in the soul by an independent outside agency, whereas affective prayer remains always dependent in its results and according to its definition upon the activity of the praying soul. Affective prayer of simplicity, or of active recollection, attains to the very threshold of the higher passive states of contemplation.

And now the question: can the Breviary serve as a useful instrument for souls that have reached the affective state?

I. Objections:

1. Since by the very definition affective prayer is so highly simplified, why wish to intrude all sorts of considerations which by their number and character will only prove a hindrance? It would be retrogression to a lower grade of prayer.

2. The soul that has reached the stage of affective prayer has but one desire: to close all books and to be content with a few fervent affections experienced again and again. Having made progress in the right direction, why begin all over again?

3. In affective prayer fervor needs to have free rein. The Breviary will not serve, for it is cold and formal and it is precisely not apt to encourage sentiment and imagination.

II. The opinion of saintly and devout souls:

Before dealing with these objections, let us consult the opinion of some who have experience both of affective prayer and of the Breviary. Here are some examples and thoughts well worth pondering:

St. Augustine: "*Psalterium meum, gaudium meum—* My Psalter is my joy."[1] And again: "How did I weep, in Thy hymns and canticles, touched to the quick by the voices of Thy Church so sweetly singing. The voices flowed into mine ears, and the truth distilled into my heart, whence the affections of my devotion overflowed."[2]

St. Athanasius: "It seems to me that the psalms should be as a mirror to him who chants them; in which he will recognize himself and the peculiar sentiments of his own soul, and in such spirit will he chant the psalms."

St. Bernard speaks of the delight which he experienced in dwelling upon the psalms, the tenderness of a word, the sweetness of a phrase (*"jucunda ruminatio psalmorum . . . ruminantes intra nosmetipsos suave verbum, eloquium dulce"*).[3]

St. Teresa: "For some years now I have derived the greatest spiritual consolation whenever I have heard or read certain phrases of the Canticle of Solomon (in the Breviary), so that even though the Spanish translation of the Latin text is not entirely clear, I have felt myself prompted to recollection and moved to devotion more than when I have read good books of piety which I found quite easy to understand."[4]

Bossuet: "Indeed, to grow old and at last to die in this holy habit (of enjoying the psalms) is all that one can wish for, it is the height of our desire, it is very bliss."[5]

Newman: "The day when I came to know and love the Breviary I count as a turning point in my life."[6]

[1] *In psal. 137*, v. 3.
[2] *Confessions*, IX, VI.
[3] *Sermo 6, in vig. Nativitatis.*
[4] *Prologue to Conceptos.*
[5] Letter dedicating to his clergy his commentary on the Psalms.
[6] *Letters and Correspondence*, Vol. II, p. 158; *Tracts for the Times*, No. 75; *Apologia pro Vita Sua*, p. 74.

Pius X: "Who is there that does not feel himself moved by the numerous passages of the psalms where time and again the immense majesty of God is sung in the sublimest terms? . . . Who is not filled with admiration at hearing the psalmist now recount the great gifts received from the divine munificence . . . and now unfold the truths of heavenly wisdom? And who, finally, does not feel his heart vibrate with love at the image of Christ so faithfully portrayed, of Christ whose voice St. Augustine (in Ps. 42, n. 1) heard in all the psalms, now chanting praises and now exclaiming in grief, telling of joys unhoped for and of sorrows presently endured."[1]

Reypens, S.J.: "My Breviary is to me as a field of clover, a meadow starred with flowers; and like the bee I plunge and hide therein; I am bathed in honey and drink the heavenly nectar in the sunlight of grace."[2]

Msgr. Waffelaert: "Nothing so nourishes the spirit of prayer, nothing is better proof of such spirit, nothing a richer source thereof, than the daily recitation of the Hour-prayers; so that the divine Office may well be called the sacrament of prayer."[3]

In the same way, all devout souls who on the one hand have some experience of affective prayer and on the other are familiar with the Breviary, will bear witness to the fact that the two are closely related.

Evidence of this may be found in certain works of spiritual writers, such as the *Exercises* of St. Gertrude. Herself an adept in affective prayer which in some of her pages springs directly from the divine Office, in one case

[1] *Divino Afflatu*, cited in Beauduin, *Liturgy the Life of the Church*, p. 66.

[2] *Poesies*.

[3] Callewaert, *De Brevarii Romani Liturgia*, p. 18.

her joy expands into a psalm and in another a psalm leads her on into loving colloquy (see especially the sixth Exercise).

Louis de Blois writes: "I prefer by all counts to experience the sweet savor of a psalm even though I do not understand it perfectly, rather than to work out its exact meaning and to miss the inward relish of it."[1]

And what may we imagine were the affective intuitions of a St. John Baptist de la Salle who never recited the Office save with his head uncovered in reverence, or of a St. John Vianney who always recited the Office before the tabernacle.

III. Reply to objections:

1. *Why intrude into affective prayer the many discursive elements of the Breviary?*

In recommending the use of the Breviary by souls who have reached the stage of affective prayer, we have no intention to intrude these many discursive elements. It is true that affective prayer does show an increasing simplification of the discursive processes and a predominance of will affections over reasoning activities. When a soul has reached this stage it may well be left to rest there. Why oblige such a one to resume the labor "of drawing water from the well by force of arm," as St. Teresa says?

However, we think that the Breviary contains something more than its discursive elements. The divine Office is a prayer of praise. This in fact is its specific character. And hence it contains an abundance of affective elements.

We do not mean to say that these affective impulses must be many in number in a given case, for that would in fact impede the soul. In meditating, for example, on

[1] *Canon Vitae Spirit.*, C. XVIII, 5.

the Office of Easter day, one who has advanced to the stage of affective prayer will proceed quite differently from what he did while still on the discursive level. In the latter case he may have paused to consider the symbolic meanings which St. Gregory attaches to the aromatic spices, the right side and the left side of the tomb, or the fear inspired by the angel. But now in the affective state he may simply dwell in the general feeling of the Easter joy which is diffused throughout the Office. The impulse may spring from the phrase: "Christ is risen," or perhaps from the single word "Alleluia." And then, as he follows through the Office the recurrence of the Alleluia, the encounter of the antiphons and the oration and each *Gloria Patri* will kindle new outbursts of joy, for these affective elements of the Breviary are, as St. Teresa says, "like bits of wood cast upon the fire." And in this way the joy may catch upon this or that phrase which suddenly may take on some personal meaning for the soul engrossed in it. For example, the antiphon: "I laid me down and slept; and I awoke, for the Lord sustained me," may arouse a sense of contrition for sin and of joy in the pardon flowing from the merits of the paschal Lamb. Or the antiphon: "I have asked the Father, alleluia; and He hath given me the nations, alleluia, for mine inheritance, alleluia," may stir the soul to jubilant admiration at the triumph of Christ the King.

2. *In the state of affective prayer the soul has no further need of books and desires rather to close them all.*

It is true that affective prayer is less dependent upon a manual than is discursive prayer. Why teach one to walk who has already learned to fly?

However, it would be presumptious to imagine that the soul arrived at this state can dispense with books altogether. Affective prayer, simplified though it is, still remains active prayer; that is, still dependent upon the soul's activity. And are we to understand that these affections do not need to be replenished? All activity implies expenditure. The soul cannot draw indefinitely upon its own resources.

Affective prayer is described by spiritual writers as a succession of impulses along the same line, the diagram of which shows a rise and fall. The dominant thought need not be always at its height. The process may be compared to a fire which flames up at intervals when new fuel is added. In such way the soul pursuing the theme of the liturgy is prompted again and again by the affective elements of the Breviary.

We do not mean to say that, if God has disposed you to affective prayer, you are obliged to take in all the affective elements contained in a given Office. You are not obliged to do that in discursive prayer or meditation, and hence certainly not in affective prayer. It is quite sufficient to choose here and there, to gather freely like the bee throughout the parts of the Office. And if you find a flower particularly rich in honey, you may linger there, even at that one place alone, without feeling obliged to any further search.

3. *Affective devotion must have free rein; the Breviary is too formal and has little room for sentiment.*

We have already considered this objection in speaking of discursive meditation. In both cases it is without foundation. Certainly you will not find in the Breviary that dubious sentimentality which we often find in certain manuals where piety is touched with romance. Nor does the Breviary give expression to highly individualized sentiment. Liturgical prayer is always collective and is not immediately concerned with this particular person and this particular moment. Each individual is expected to make his own personal application. "The daily Office," says Mauriac, "contains an appropriate message for each particular person."[1]

Leaving aside then mere romantic and egotistic sentimentality, what a wonderful store of true human sentiment is contained in the Breviary. Jubilation, contrition, admiration, enthusiasm, affliction, disillusionment, and even indignation, all these are there; and especially there is love singing on every page. The examples we have quoted are proof sufficient, and we need not dwell any longer on this objection which really is made in advance by those who have not yet ventured the experience.

IV. Positive advantages:

From the point of view of affective prayer, the Breviary offers the following advantages:

1. *It increases our spiritual sensibility.*

It enlarges our vision, so that we are no longer limited to our personal horizon, which we soon find to be a narrow one. We are no longer concerned merely with our personal sentiments, our own joys and sorrows, but we learn that there are greater things in which we may both rejoice and grieve. As we go on living the Breviary, the passion as well as the glory of Christ envelope us, His joys and His sorrows, His abjection and His triumph become our own experience as we dwell upon them. The use of the Breviary develops in us the spirit of praise and this sense of ceaseless praise is itself a state of affective prayer.

To draw inspiration in this way from the Breviary is truly *"sentire cum Ecclesia,"* to live in the mind of the

[1] *Joies et douleurs du chretien,* p. 119.

Church. In the Office of Easter, for example, our joy in Christ's victory is not for our own sake alone but for that of the entire mystical body. We experience a kind of collective, social joy in the mystery of regeneration. Similarly during Lent, as we daily recite the *Miserere*, we are moved to contrition for sin, our own sins and the sins of all mankind which caused the sufferings of our dear Savior.

2. *It introduces great variety into affective life.*

Devout souls frequently complain of monotony in their prayer-life. The fact is that the range of anyone's personal sentiment is rather limited. The use of the Breviary increases the range very distinctly. It has one series of affective elements belonging to Advent and another to Lent and still another to the Easter season. During Advent the lessons from Isaias awaken a feeling of happy expectancy; the Office of Passiontide fills the soul with a sense of compassion; and altogether different again are the sentiments proper to the season of Pentecost. Thus our prayer is protected against monotony.

Moreover the Office contains a great variety of parts which are of affective character, the hymns, doxologies, the Alleluia, the majority of the versicles and responsories and antiphons. When the exercise of affective prayer follows immediately upon the vocal recitation, these serve as an excellent preparation of the soul, disposing it to a definite affective state and introducing it into a specific affective environment.

Furthermore, from the private point of view, the entire range of individual sentiment is represented in the Breviary in formulas that are at once human and profound. Consider especially the psalter: Psalm 83 as expressing joy, Psalm 22, confidence, Psalm 41, desire, Psalm 139, fear, Psalm 50, contrition, Psalm 68, anguish, Psalm 87, sorrow, Psalm 129, hope. In fact the psalms offer no end of inspiration for affective prayer.

Raoul de Tongres has said that the psalms are like the manna of the desert, suitable to every taste: *"Habent affectum omnium orationum."*[1] One may observe how certain saints made use of these formulas and found inspiration in them.

3. *It safeguards the sincerity of affective prayer.*

In speaking of discursive prayer we averted to the danger of artificiality. All the more in the case of affective prayer where there is still less room for the conventional and where it is important to hold to the middle way between the two extremes of the formal and stereotyped on the one hand and cheap sentimentality on the other.

If one follows the Breviary properly, its variety will obviate the danger of formalism, and on the other hand the Breviary is as far removed as possible from cheap sentimentality. And if its prayer formulas do seem somewhat severe and impersonal, we ourselves supply what is lacking in this respect by our application of them to ourselves, while at the same time their general style and consecrated character prevent us from carrying the individualizing process to the extreme of sentimentalism.

"The tendency of the liturgy," says Dom Ryelandt, "is precisely to develop a sincere disposition in souls." And he adds: "The Church in furnishing us with the formulas of her official prayer, aims to establish in us the same holy dispositions which these formulas express, interior sentiments of humility and contrition, affective movements of love and praise and gratitude and of union with the divine

---

[1] Quoted by Dom Ryelandt in his paper, *Breviaire et Meditation*, at the Liturgical Week at Maredsous in 1912; *Cours et Conf. des Semaines Liturgiques*, 1913, p. 181.

will. '*Quod os dicit cor sapit*—the heart treasures what the lips utter.'

"Now, is not this the aim of all the methodical meditation manuals? Do they not seek to elicit, by their customary considerations of three points, movements of affection and good resolutions? The liturgy tends directly to the same end, but by a shorter way, by immediate suggestion of the aforesaid dispositions of the soul."[1]

We may quote, finally, a passage from Cassian referring to the psalms:

"For if we have experience of the very state of mind in which each psalm was sung and written, we become like their authors and anticipate the meaning rather than follow it. We gather the force of the words before we really know them. We remember what has happened to us, and what is happening in daily assaults when the thoughts of them come over us, and while we sing them we call to mind all that our carelessness has brought upon us, or our earnestness has secured, or divine Providence has granted, or the promptings of the foe have deprived us of, or slippery and subtle forgetfulness has carried off, or human weakness has brought about, or thoughtless ignorance has cheated us of.

"For all these feelings we find expressed in the psalms, so that by seeing whatever happens as in a clear mirror, we understand it better. And so instructed by our feelings as our teachers, we lay hold of it as something not merely heard but actually seen, and, as if it were not committed to memory but implanted in the very nature of things. We are affected from the very bottom of the heart, so that we get at the meaning not by reading the text but by experience anticipating it."[2]

[1] Ryelandt, *loc. cit.*
[2] *Conferences*, PNF., Vol. XI (second series), p. 408.

V. Practical applications:

In the case of affective prayer less need be said about method. For the soul in this stage has a greater sense of liberty and definite directions might prove to be a hindrance. Therefore certain souls especially disposed to affective prayer, like St. Teresa, have never been able to accommodate themselves to ready-made methods. This is no valid argument against the employment of methods in prayer, as some have tried to make out in opposition to them. It merely shows that purely discursive prayer does not satisfy certain souls, feminine souls especially, and that they should be left more free to move Godward by the promptings of their heart.

We should add that not all the elements of the Office have equal value from the affective point of view. Some of the lessons certainly do possess the power to inspire the sentiments corresponding to the mystery of the day; and certain psalms are extraordinarily apt to heighten devotion. But in proportion as affective prayer increases in simplicity, the soul is likely to content itself with the shorter elements found in the hymns, antiphons, responsories, versicles, and even in a simple exclamation like the Alleluia.

First Example: We shall borrow this first example from Dom Ryelandt[1]:

"Suppose that in reciting the Office one says to himself with all his heart these words which his lips utter: '*A custodia matutina usque ad noctem speret Israel in Domino*—From the morning watch even until night let Israel hope in the Lord.' And supposing that at the end of the Office or of the psalm the soul continues to cherish this thought and, in order to overcome distractions and to guard the flame of love and confidence which these words have in-

[1]Ryelandt, *op. cit.*, p. 137.

spired, repeats them softly from time to time, or utters some brief phrase of the same tenor—this certainly will be excellent prayer.

"One may pray thus with various other phrases for one's inspiration. Thus the feeling of resignation in the hands of God may spring from the words: '*Jacta super Dominum curam tuam et Ipse te enutriet*—Cast thy care upon the Lord and He will sustain thee'; or, '*Obumbrasti super caput meum in die belli*—Thou hast overshadowed my head in the day of battle.' Or it may be some phrase that spurs one to fidelity or that prompts one to repentance or to pure love: '*Quid mihi est in coelo, et a te quid volui super terram*—For what have I in heaven and what besides Thee do I desire upon earth?' Read the penitential psalms and you will be conscious of a lingering note of compunction in the depths of your soul which will prompt you to say with the heart even more than with the lips: '*Domine, ne in furore tuo arguas me*—O Lord, rebuke me not in Thy wrath'; or again: '*Miserere mei, Deus, secundum magnam misericordiam tuam*—Have mercy upon me, O God, according to Thy great mercy.' These interior sentiments which the psalms or other parts of the liturgy inspire are true prayer indeed. Be they the plaints of a suffering heart, or the yielding of complete confidence, or expressions of pure love, or resolutions to do God's will always, they are precious values in spiritual life."

We might go on indefinitely with examples of this kind. Meditation on the formula: "*Deus in adjutorium meum intende*—O God, come to mine aid," which occurs at the beginning of each Hour, when meditated in the affective way, suggests to Cassian a whole series of affective impulses corresponding to the various circumstances in which the soul feels the need of God.[1]

[1]*Conferences, ibid.*, p. 405.

We may mention also Psalm 118 which has for its theme the beauty of the divine law and of the will of God. It is replete with formulas prompting to affective prayer. Pascal found this psalm especially appealing to his devotion.

Second Example: the antiphons of the Office of the Immaculate Conception.

These antiphons, occurring both in Lauds and Vespers, are five in number. Taking them all together, one may think of them as a hymn of five stanzas chanted in Mary's honor in the high courts of heaven.

I. We may imagine the first antiphon as spoken by the almighty God Himself. The Holy Trinity, looking upon Mary, is well pleased. "Thou art all fair," says the Father; and the Son exclaims: "O Mary," repeating the name so often spoken by His human lips; "and the original stain is not in thee," says the Holy Spirit, the worker of this prodigy.

II. The angels chant the second antiphon: "Thy garment is white as snow," sing the Seraphim, the spirits of the pure heights of contemplation; and the Cherubim, the spirits of ardor, aflame with love, reply in the counterphrase: "and thy face is like the sun."

III. The third antiphon is intoned by the apostles: "Thou art the glory of Jerusalem," both the earthly and the heavenly Jerusalem; the white-robed army of martyrs pursues the strain: "Thou art the joy of Israel," of the Church for which the martyrs have gladly shed their blood; and the great host of confessors completes the antiphon: "Thou art the honor of our people," of the race of which we all are born, human and mortal like ourselves, the chosen one who marks the beginning of our triumph.

IV. The holy women, the matrons of the heavenly throng, sing the fourth antiphon: "Blessed are thou, O Virgin Mary, above all women upon earth."

V. The hymn ends with the fifth antiphon, sung by the virgins who invite us also to follow with them in the fragrant retinue of their queen: "Draw us, O immaculate Virgin, we will run after thee in the odor of thine ointments."

Third Example: the Office for the feast of St. Agatha.

This example is still more complex. It embraces the entire Office of this feast (February 5) considered throughout as an example of affective prayer. The affective elements in this particular Office may be reduced to three principal ones which suggest themselves quite spontaneously:

a) A general sense of joy;

b) A more particular sense of admiration;

c) The excellence of the virtue of purity.

a) *Joy*: 1. with Christ whose external glory is increased through the merits of this virgin-martyr; 2. with the Church to whose honor St. Agatha redounds; 3. with St. Agatha herself in her triumph.

In this spirit of joy we recite or chant the invitatory antiphon and psalm, in which the words *"exultemus"* and *"jubilemus"* apply directly to our present mood. The feeling of joy is sustained throughout the hymn in which we sing of Agatha's victory in her martyrdom.

She herself gives expression to her joy in the first nocturn: "I will give glory to Thee, O Lord and King, and I will praise Thee, O God, my Savior. Thou hast preserved my body from destruction, from the oppression of the flame, and in the midst of the fire I was not burned. My soul shall praise the Lord even unto death."

b) *Admiration*: at the power of God and at the virtue of St. Agatha.

The power of God: admiration expressed in the oration: "O God, who amidst the other wondrous works of Thy power hast bestowed the victory of martyrdom even on the weaker sex; mercifully grant that we who celebrate the heavenly birth-day of blessed Agatha, Thy virgin and martyr, may, by following her example advance in the way that leadeth to Thee."

The virtue of St. Agatha: expressed throughout the entire Office in the psalms. It is the purpose of the antiphons to indicate the particular sentiment in which the several psalms are to be recited. For example, in the second nocturn Psalm 8, "O Lord, our Lord, how admirable is Thy name in the whole world," receives a special application to St. Agatha by means of the preceding antiphon· "Agatha went to prison with great joy and exultation like a guest to a banquet, and recommended her struggle to the Lord in prayer." This is as beautiful as any deed of valor. One is reminded of the Mexican priests who fell before the bullets of their executioners with the cry: "Long live Christ the King," and one is moved to repeat the words of the psalm, "O Lord, our Lord, how admirable is Thy name in the whole world"—and throughout all ages.

Thus the series of antiphons which recount the modest and undisturbed replies of St. Agatha while so hideously maltreated by the cruel Quintianus sustain our feeling of admiration.

c) *The excellence of purity*: This Office is that of a virgin and hence the thought of purity suggests itself from the very beginning. For the sake of this virtue St. Agatha sacrificed her life. Her strength appears in her guarding of her purity. The purity of Christ, her divine Bridegroom, is ever in the background while she speaks in the antiphons: "O Lord, Thou hast seen how I have fought and how I have run in the race; but because I would not obey the commands of the magistrates they ordered that I be tortured in my breasts" (3 Noct., Ant. 2). "Because of my chastity they ordered that I be stretched upon the rack; help me, O Lord, in the torture of my breasts" (3 Noct., Ant. 3).

Having entered into the prison where she was to die "she stretched forth her hands to God and said: 'O Lord, who hast made me to overcome the cruelty of the executioners, may it please Thee that I should attain unto Thy mercy" (Resp. 7). "Who art thou who comest to heal my wounds? I am an apostle of Christ; have no fear of me, my daughter. He hath sent me to thee whom thy soul and thy pure heart have loved" (Resp. 3).

PART FOUR

THE BREVIARY AS A BASIS OF CONTEMPLATIVE PRAYER

I. Objections:

There are no objections at all coming from the contemplatives themselves. For all these whom God conducts in the highest ways of prayer have a keen desire for the inspired sources and find delight in liturgical prayer and particularly in the divine Office.

It is possible, however, to imagine two theoretical objections:

1. Contemplative prayer is by its definition something secret, with no intermediary between the soul and God who manifests Himself to the soul in this stage of prayer either according to certain modes or without any mode in a purely spiritual way. How then can you wish to introduce an intermediary which will only interfere in these direct relations? There is no place here for a manual.

2. Contemplative prayer is essentially private prayer by the very reason of the secret character of these exalted relations between the soul and God. Therefore it is said to be mystical. And how then can you propose a manual of official prayer, one that is concerned with official and collective relations, that is to say, public relations with God? Therefore a liturgical manual is decidedly out of place here.

In addition to these two objections, there are two more possible arguments that may be advanced:

3. Do not the actual facts sustain the aforesaid objections? For they show that in the exercise of contemplative prayer the Breviary text is not only useless but a positive hindrance. Thus, St. Joseph of Cupertino was never able to recite the Office. Though he kept paging his Breviary all day, he had never finished it by night, for at every attempt an irresistible concentration overpowered him and suspended the action of his faculties. St. Philip Neri was not able to recite the Office except by alternating with a companion. A dispensation from the Breviary was obtained for St. Ignatius because he was not able to get through with it. And does not our Lord seem to discourage the use of a book by souls in this high stage of prayer when He says, for example, to St. Teresa: "My child, I shall be your book?"

4. The teaching of the mystics seems to be in conformity with such facts. Speaking of the prayer of quietude, St. Teresa says: "At such times speech of any kind, vocal or mental, is fatiguing to the soul, whose desire is simply to love."[1] And St. Catherine of Siena represents the voice of God as saying to her: "As soon as the soul becomes aware of My approach let vocal prayer be put aside and resumed later if time permits when the mental prayer is finished. But exception must be made in regard to the divine Office which clerics and religious are obliged to recite. If at the time assigned for this recitation they feel their soul attracted and uplifted by desire, they should make provision to say the Office before or after. Thus with exercise of perseverance the soul will learn the secret of

[1] Letter to Father Alvarez.

true prayer and will be nourished with the blood of My only Son."[1]

II. The opinion and the example of the mystics:

In his *Retreat for Eight Days* Bourdaloue devotes the meditations of the third day to the divine Office, and does not hesitate to say: "This prayer alone, if performed as it should be, would suffice for the attainment of perfection."[2] And all the contemplatives agree in this opinion.

St. Joseph of Cupertino was once asked by a bishop how the latter might best succeed in promoting the sanctity of his clergy, and the saint replied: "Let your Lordship see to it that your priests celebrate the Mass and recite the Breviary devoutly."

The fact is that the mystics valued the Breviary most highly as a means for the attainment of perfection, and their writings show that they always considered it a great aid in every stage of their prayer-life and never found it a hindrance or an obstacle. On the contrary, it is quite true to say that they clung to it.

St. Ignatius was so moved during his recitation of the Office that the flood of his tears threatened to impair his vision. His companions obtained a dispensation for him without his knowledge. But he refused to avail himself of it and, begging God to moderate his emotion, he continued his recitation of the Breviary to which he was so devoted.[3]

It should hardly be necessary to cite the example of St. Gertrude, the illustrious Benedictine nun, whose contemplative prayer was based entirely upon the divine Office and flourished in conjunction with it.

[1]*Dialogue*, C. 66, 224-6.
[2]Hoornaert, *Le Breviaire*, p. 56.
[3]Hoornaert, *ibid.*, p. 69.

No doubt at times the mystics passed beyond their ordinary depth and were carried out upon deep waters and toward the ocean of mystical revelation. But they reverted again to the liturgical text which never failed to steady and sustain them.

The love which St. Benedict Labre had for the Office dated from his youth, says his biographer. "But his habit of reciting the Office daily, from the breviary which he carried about with him on his mendicant tours, dated from the time of his sojourn at the abbey of La Trappe. Since he was not obliged to conform to choir rules, he would pause in the middle of a psalm, over some phrase, over some word perhaps, for the mystic impulse cannot be controlled, while his spirit soared on open wing throughout the wide range of the Scriptures. In most such cases he no longer dwelt within the sphere where the soul finds aid in speech. With hands crossed upon his breast and eyelids closed, now and again a sigh escaped his lips as the mystery which he contemplated moved him in grief or in love. After a while he seemed to return to life, he opened his eyes and fixed them upon the tabernacle, and again took up his bulky breviary in his right hand and opened it upon his left arm."[1]

That illustrious contemplative, the Cure of Ars, once exclaimed while reciting his Breviary, and kneeling on the hard tiles of the sacristy floor: "What a blessing it is to be able to refresh oneself a little." "He found delight in the beauty of the psalms," writes the Abbé Trochu,[2] "and though he had only a limited knowledge of Latin, he was able by a special grace to perceive the deep meaning of them." "When I think of these beautiful prayers," he once

[1] Grolleau, *La Vie et les Oeuvres de quelques grands Saints.* T. II, St. Benoît Jos. Labre, p. 246.
[2] *Le Cure d'Ars*, p. 384.

said, "I am tempted to exclaim: 'O happy fault': for if David had not wept for his sins we would not have his psalms." His love for the psalms was extended to the volume that contained them. "He loved his breviary so much," says the Abbé Tailhades, "that in his daily round of duty he nearly always carried it under his arm. When I asked him why he did this, he replied: 'My breviary is my faithful companion; I would not go anywhere without it.'" We are told about his appearance when he recited it. "His countenance," says an eye-witness, "reflected the deep sentiments of his soul; his lips seemed to relish the thoughts upon which his mind dwelt; his eyes lighted up and sparkled; he appeared to breathe an atmosphere more pure than that of earth, and having shut out the din of the world, he heard only the voice of the Holy Spirit."[1]

III. Reply to objections:

1. *A manual is out of place in contemplative prayer.*

Let it be noted that we are speaking now of the Breviary not as a manual of contemplative prayer but as a basis or a point of departure for contemplation. It is true that the book of the contemplative is God Himself, or the divine Realities, according to the words of Christ to St. Teresa. But certainly to deny all books to contemplatives would be a great mistake, quite as if one were to consider them as incapable *a priori* of all vocal prayer. St. Teresa says, in speaking of prayer of quietude: "In this state mental prayer should not be abandoned altogether, nor even vocal prayers from time to time, if the soul has the desire and the strength to recite them."[2]

We think, therefore, that even in the case of contemplatives it is not a mistake to advise a book which may

[1] *Ibid.*, p. 385.
[2] *Vie,* 15.

serve as a support, or at least as a point of departure for their mystic prayer. And contemplatives have full right even to become absorbed in it. When the Lord sees fit He will take the book from them.

2. *Contemplative prayer is essentially private; why then urge the use of liturgical prayers which are essentially collective?*

What is the meaning of the term, private prayer? If contemplative prayer is said to be private by reason of the intimate, secret or mystical character of the relations between the soul and God which it implies, we admit that it is private in that sense. Or, if private prayer is taken to mean that kind of prayer which a person says in his heart, in silence, even though a group of persons are so engaged at the same time, and in contradistinction to prayer which is said aloud and in common, again we admit that the former is properly called private prayer, and so indeed St. Benedict speaks of it in his Rule. But if one means to set contemplation in opposition to the official prayer of the Church and to maintain that there are two opposite kinds of prayer, one private and interior and the other public and exterior, we refuse to grant this use of the terms private and public as meaning two mutually exclusive things. To represent public, liturgical prayer as something merely external would be to betray a very inadequate understanding of it and to do it a grave injustice. "The official worship of the Church (the liturgy therefore) is the exercise not only of the exterior priesthood of Christ but also *and above all* of His interior priesthood. The liturgy is primarily the interior religion of the Son of God towards His Father and secondarily His exterior religion."[1] In order

[1] Lefebvre. *La Religion d'Amour*, p. 48.

that spirit may accord with voice, private or interior prayer must accompany public prayer, just as the soul must be united with the body if there is to be life and movement. And if the private prayer is also contemplative, the life and movement of the exterior, collective, liturgical prayer will be all the more fruitful. The two aspects, interior and exterior, of the one same prayer are far from being in opposition.

Since then it is quite permissible to offer to contemplatives some sort of book to sustain their union with God, as we have shown in dealing with the first objection, we can think of none better than the liturgical books, and notably the Breviary.

3. *The facts are opposed to it.*

The general assertion that facts taken as a whole prove the use of books to be incompatible with contemplative prayer is to be rejected as false.

It is necessary here to make a distinction as to these facts.

That certain states of contemplative prayer, which, moreover, may be said to be accidental, are incompatible with the use of the Breviary at a given moment, we readily grant. The states of ligature and ecstacy and all the various degrees of faculty suspension naturally prohibit the use at the time of formulas other than those adapted to the state, or perhaps of all formulas. And many instances of ligature and ecstacy can be cited in which it would be annoying and useless to impose ready-made prayers on the contemplative.

But contemplative prayer is not limited to these states nor to these accidental phenomena. On the contrary, the very highest state in the contemplative life, that of the spiritual marriage or transforming union, shows us, once it is attained, subjects capable of attending to all their duties, and consequently to their obligation in regard to the official prayer and to the recitation of the Breviary, and all without any loss of the contemplative union. St. Gertrude, St. John Vianney and the venerable Marie de l'Incarnation are typical examples of this.

As for the states inferior to ecstacy, such as the prayer of passive recollection or certain states of quietude, the facts make it equally plain that the contemplative in these states is better able to attend to vocal prayers when these are liturgical and said in common.

Finally, over against all such objections as have been considered here, we can place this one supreme fact: from the lips of the dying Christ in the mystic state of anguish and agony, we hear the murmur of the psalms and the distinct verse of Psalm 21: "Why hast Thou forsaken me?"

4. *The doctrine of the mystics is opposed to it.*

It would be a mistake to apply some of their particular assertions to the whole of contemplative prayer and to all the states of the mystical life. These assertions refer only to certain states of ligature, certain rather rare moments of faculty suspension in which indeed it would be useless for the soul undergoing the divine action to try to cling to anything other than what God Himself wishes to instil. St. Teresa says this quite distinctly. And when St. Catherine of Siena says: "If at the time assigned for this recitation (of the Breviary) they feel their soul attracted and uplifted by desire, they should make provision to say the Office before or after," these words are to be taken to mean that if at the time for reciting or meditating the Hour-prayers they feel an irresistible divine attraction, it is useless to struggle against it; and instead of prolonging a dull and irksome prayer, continually distracted, full of interruptions and in the end definitely cut short, it is better not to resist the divine impulse and to arrange to recite or meditate the Hour-prayers before or after these moments of intense concentration.

IV. The excellence of liturgical prayer as related to contemplation:

1. "The soul living by means of the liturgy of each day and of each hour under the influence of the eternal Highpriest, becomes the voice of the Church and therefore of the Holy Spirit, uttering with lips and heart the psalmody and sacred lessons which the Holy Spirit in times past breathed into the prophets, given over in faith and love to the Mother of saints in whom circulates the great stream of supernatural life; is it not likely that the soul living thus in intimate converse with God through all the hours of the day and night will be able to discover in this habitual union the ardent desire and the divine strength to conemplate Him?"[1]

Indeed, the soul favored with the graces of contemplaplative prayer will be sensible of the divine presence in reading and meditating with the Breviary more than with any other book; more really conscious of the radiance of God's face; with lips opened, as the preliminary prayer says, "to bless His holy name," with attention fixed upon the liturgical formulas and through them upon God, "to be enlightened in mind and enkindled in affections"; reminded throughout the Office of the presence of the Holy Trinity, for example in the *Gloria Patri* at the end of every psalm. The Office, like the Mass, is above all a hymn to the Holy Trinity. Its structure is trinitarian throughout by the grouping of its elements in threes.

[1] Beauduin, *Liturgy the Life of the Church*, p. 74.

The soul thus favored with the graces of divine union and endowed with keener perceptivity, will recognize in the Office the *epithalamium* of the Church, the nuptial song of the Bride extolling the divine Bridegroom in words that are her own. The soul's own feebleness of expression is no obstacle here. This prayer is worthy of Him, nor can anything better be said to Him, for these are the very words of the Holy Spirit.

2. All the great contemplatives tell us that in the mystic state, understanding that term in the widest sense as including all forms of ligature and ecstacy and faculty suspension, the soul receives from God extraordinary and profound enlightenments in regard to the meaning of Scriptural texts. These texts, because they are either the very words of the Holy Spirit or the voice of the Church, are ordinarily chosen by God to be the vehicle of secret revelations which He wishes to grant to these souls.

These enlightenments represent new aspects of divine truth, for the Holy Spirit is multiform. In reading the books of the mystics we are often struck by the very personal interpretations of certain words of the Scriptures that we find in them. The mystics do not offer these interpretations as the discursive exegetes do, as reasoned opinions; they speak in a way that would seem naive were it not for the supernatural certitude that they display. They say: "The Holy Spirit says," or "God has told us," etc.

In addition to the fact that the Breviary furnishes to contemplatives wonderful texts which serve as the direct vehicles of an interior voice, what marvelous reminders of past experiences it must hold for them! Some verse of a psalm that one day revealed its meaning in a flash of light; some lesson recalling a grace received on a certain day of the liturgical year; some phrase which brought strength and consolation in time of distress; some psalm that never fails to bring its inspiration and to expand their heart with the mighty influx of divine Love.

Garden of delights, full of enrapturing surprises and of unforgettable memories, must not the Breviary be for contemplatives above all others the most precious of books!

3. The prayers of the Breviary are well adapted to the various states of the contemplative life. We shall consider these states in the order marked out by St. Teresa:

a) *Prayer of recollection:*

This is the threshold of the passive states; the soul is recollected here in the passive sense, that is, retired inwardly rather than recollected by positive effort.

A quiet and affective recitation of the Breviary is an excellent means to sustain the soul in this state. A psalm or a lesson is read very slowly with some reflection on its meaning; not, however, a reflection which becomes discursive, but a unified attention, a simple regard, upon some salient thought, be it of love, of contrition, of hope, of desire, a series of images which one reviews in passing, with pauses now and then to dwell silently on this or that one. In this way one may read in the joy peculiar to Christmas, or listen to the chant of the first lesson of Matins for that day; or on the feast of the dedication of a church one may linger over the hymn, *Coelestis urbs*, and all the while continuing in the state of passive recollection.

b) *Prayer of quietude:*

In this state the soul reposes in a deeper silence. "In these happy moments," says St. Teresa, "it is impossible to doubt the presence of God within oneself."[1] This divine presence groups the higher faculties of the soul into

[1] *Vie*, 15.

unity and maintains them in a quiet and simple attention to God which the soul is unable to disturb.

One simple verse of a psalm, a mere fragment of a phrase is sufficient for the soul in this state, dwelling upon a word in close union with God. For example, in the Christmas season, in reciting the Canticle of Isaias (XII, 1-6, II Lauds), kneeling in spirit at the foot of the crib, and continuing in quietude while the lips and even the imagination are astir, what meaning then do these words take on: *"Ecce Salvator meus; fiducialiter agam et non timebo*—Behold, God is my Savior; I shall deal confidently and shall not fear." *"Haurietis aqua in gaudio de fontibus Salvatoris*—You shall draw water with joy out of the Savior's fountains." *"Exulta et lauda habitatio Sion*—Rejoice and praise, O thou habitation of Sion."

If at such times the soul is not prevented from vocal prayer by ecstacy or ligature, the psalmody is like a clear and constant breeze which refreshes the soul in its quietude and which is described by one of the mystics as laden with the perfume of roses. In this state of quietude the encounter of certain words may produce transports without yet disturbing the peace of the soul, or there may come impulses of jubilation which find expression in ardent colloquy or perhaps in song. These experiences are called "praying quietude" and "quietude of jubilation."[1]

c) *Prayer of union:*

In this state the utterances of the Holy Spirit in the divine Office produce an impression so deep and powerful as to imbue as it were the very substance of the soul. In these moments of intense union, when faith expands in marvelous profusion, the soul feels itself become the very voice of the Holy Spirit, or better, of the Church. The

[1] Poulain, *The Graces of Interior Prayer*, pp. 183-4.

slightest lingering upon one of these utterances is apt to produce a concentration so great that the ligature becomes irresistible.

The mystics emerge from these experiences enriched with enlightenments in regard to the meaning of the texts. And thus we have certain glowing commentaries from their pens, such as the *Conceptions of Divine Love* of St. Teresa.

d) *The spiritual marriage*:

In this state the soul is totally united with God, in its faculties and in its substance, and not in a transitory way and in certain instances but permanently. The Office, far from being an obstacle, is now the appropriate channel of the soul's prayer. Freed henceforth, at least normally, from the violent phenomena, the mystic reverts with greater joy than ever to the beloved Breviary. The Office is now in full truth the loving and untroubled converse of the Bridegroom and the Bride. Intimately united with Christ, the supreme priest, the soul's praises are merged in His. The voices of Christ and of the Church and of the soul in its mystical marriage blend in perfect harmony. And the words by which the Church here on earth exercises the priestly function of Christ in prayer will always be preferred by such a soul, willing to exchange all the formulas in the world, and especially its own personal ones, for the least word of the liturgy.

4. The words of the divine Office, because they are more than ordinary prayer, because they are the words of the Holy Spirit and the voice of the Church, often *produce* in the soul that which they express. They are spirit and life. And they are intended for these extraordinary contemplative souls more than for any others.

They bring moments of respite to suffering souls plunged in the "night of the senses." They relieve the anguish of the "night of the spirit," coming as gleams of light to pierce the terrible darkness. They fill the soul with an insatiable divine desire. They expand in unspeakable joy. They suddenly encompass the soul in profound and ineffable peace. All these things are told to us by the mystics, over and over again. And when they speak of these things they all agree that no other prayer has such power as the liturgy to carry them into the depths of the divine union.

V. Practical applications:

It is hardly possible to reproduce an example of contemplative prayer. The essential things in the case, the light in which the contemplative soul is bathed, the ardor that moves the will and elevates the soul above itself—these are lost in any attempt to express them in words. The most that we can do here is to indicate the results of such prayer by repeating what the mystics have said regarding their experiences as associated with the Breviary and to point out some passages from that same source.

In reading what follows here it is essential to bear in mind those features of contemplative prayer which cannot be described in words.

I. *The divine Office and the states of contemplative prayer.*

The experiences of the mystics in the various states of the contemplative life are often of very delicate nature and difficult to describe. Many of the mystics have attempted to give some account of them in their treatises or in their autobiographies.

We shall not go into these matters but shall be content to point out that such states of soul often find very adequate expression in various passages in the divine Office, passages which the mystics are pleased to recognize as corresponding to their inward experiences and to employ in their efforts to give some account of these.

Nor is this fact surprising. Does not the Breviary contain many passages taken from the writings of great mystics, such as St. Augustine, St. Bernard, St. Bonaventure, and above all, the Psalmist? These writers have well expressed what they have well understood.

Let us take, for example, the state of the soul in the "dark night" whether of sense or spirit; and read Psalm 68 (Third nocturn of Matins on Thursday).

"Save me, O my God, for the waters are come in even unto my soul.

"I stick fast in the mire of the deep, and there is no sure standing.

"I am come into the depth of the sea, and a tempest hath overwhelmed me.

"I have labored with crying; my jaws have become hoarse.

"My eyes have failed, whilst I hope in my God."

Unless one understands such words as these in their relation to mystical experience, one can have only a faint idea of their meaning.

They express the mystical state of our Lord's soul in His passion, and the mystical agony of the Church, afflicted with the same divine anguish; the thirst for God who has apparently withdrawn His presence; the thirst of torturing love.

We may cite an example to show how St. John of the Cross finds this state of soul expressed in a passage in the Breviary:

"The burning fire of love, in general, is not felt at first, for it has not yet begun to burn, either because of our natural want of purity, or because the soul, not understanding its own state, has not given it a peaceful rest within itself. Sometimes, however, whether that be the case or not, a certain anxiety about God arises; and the more it grows, the more the soul feels itself touched and inflamed with the love of God, without knowing how or whence that feeling arises, except that at times this burning so inflames it that it longs earnestly after God. David in this night said of himself: '*Quia inflammatum est cor meum, et renes mei commutati sunt; et ego ad nihilum redactus sum et nescivi*—For my heart hath been inflamed, and my reins have been changed, and I am brought to nothing, and I knew not' (Ps. 72, Thursday at Terce). That is, my heart hath been inflamed in the love of contemplation; and my reins, that is, my tastes and affections also, have been changed from the sensitive to the spiritual way by this holy dryness, and in my cessation from them all; and I am brought to nothing and I knew not. The soul, as I have just said, not knowing the way it goeth, sees itself brought to nothing as to all things of heaven and earth, wherein it delighted before, and on fire with love, not knowing how.

"And because occasionally this fire of love grows in the spirit greatly, the longings of the soul for God are so deep that the very bones seem to dry up in that thirst, the bodily health to wither, the natural warmth and energies to perish in the intensity of that thirst of love. The soul feels it to be a living thirst. Such, also, was the feeling of David when he said: '*Sitivit anima mea ad Deum vivum*—My soul hath thirsted after the living God' (Ps. 41, Tuesday at Sext). It is as if he had said, my thirst is a strong, living thirst. We may say of this thirst that, being a living thirst, it kills."[1]

---

[1] *The Obscure Night*, Bk. I, Ch. XI, Lewis trans., Longmans, pp. 356-7.

Again St. John of the Cross, in explaining how in the night of the senses the soul finds God, discovers in the Psalter the answer to the mystic cry of St. Augustine: "*Noverim me, noverim te.*" "Thus out of this obscure night springs first the knowledge of oneself, and on that, as on a foundation, is built up the knowledge of God. 'Let me know myself,' saith St. Augustine, 'and I shall then know Thee.' . . . In order to show more fully how effectual is the night of sense, in its aridity and desolation, to enlighten the soul more and more, I produce the words of the Psalmist, which so clearly describe the power of this night in bringing men to the knowledge of God: '*In terra deserta et invia et inaquosa; sic in sancto apparui tibi, ut viderem virtutem tuam et gloriam tuam*—In a desert place where there is no way and no water, so in the sanctuary have I come before Thee, to see Thy power and Thy glory' (Ps. 62, Sunday at Lauds). The Psalmist does not say—and it is worthy of observation—that his previous sweetness and delight were any dispositions meet for the knowledge of the glory of God, but rather that aridity and weaning from the sensitive faculties, which are here meant by the 'barren land.' Neither does he say that his reflections and meditations on divine things, with which he was once familiar, had led him to the knowledge and contemplation of God's power, but rather his inability to meditate on God, to form reflections by the help of his imagination, which he describes by a 'land where there is no way.'"[1]

How many times do we not find in the Office expression of the desire of mystical love to be hidden away in the face of God: "*Abscondes eos in abscondito faciei tuae, a conturbatione hominum*—Thou shalt hide them in the secret of Thy face, from the disturbance of men" (Ps. 30,

[1] *Ibid.*, Ch. XII, p. 363.

Monday at Sext). Let St. John of the Cross again comment on these words:

"O my God and my life, they shall know Thee and behold Thee when Thou touchest them, who, making themselves strangers upon earth, shall purify themselves, because purity corresponds with purity. Thou the more gently touchest, the more Thou art hidden in the purified soul of those who have made themselves strangers here, hidden from the face of all creatures, and whom 'Thou shalt hide in the secret of Thy face from the disturbance of men.' O, again and again, gentle touch, which by the power of Thy subtility undoest the soul, removest it far away from every other touch whatever, and makest it Thine own; Thou which leavest behind Thee effects and impressions so pure, that the touch of everything else seems vile and low, the very sight offensive, and all relations therewith a deep affliction."[1]

Thus we see how suggestive a single verse of the psalms may be to the mystics. Is it not likely that St. John of the Cross would recall such thoughts in his recitation of the Breviary?

And what of the exclamations of love that occur so frequently throughout the Office, telling of intimate union with God: *"Quam bonus Israel Deus, his qui recto sunt corde*—How good is God to Israel, unto them that are of upright heart" (Ps. 72, Thursday at Terce). And again: *"Diligam te Domine, fortitudo mea; Dominus firmamentum et refugium meum et liberator meus*—I will love Thee, O Lord, my strength; the Lord is my firmament, my refuge and my deliverer" (Ps. 17, Monday at Matins, 2 noct.).

And the sudden outbursts of jubilation and of exulting praise: *"Quam dilecta tabernacula tua, Domine virtu-*

[1]*The Living Flame,* Stanza II, Line III, Lewis trans., Longmans. p. 242.

tum; concupiscit et deficit anima mea in atria Domini. . . . Cor et caro mea exsultaverunt in Deum vivum—How lovely are Thy tabernacles, O Lord of hosts; my soul longeth and fainteth for the courts of the Lord. . . . My heart and my flesh have rejoiced in the living God" (Ps. 83, Friday at Sext).

And the glowing admiration at the greatness of God: "*Quam magnificata sunt opera tua, Domine; omnia in sapientia fecisti*—How great are Thy works, O Lord! Thou hast made all things in wisdom" (Ps. 103, Saturday at Sext).

And the joy of Psalm 118 that extends throughout all the Minor Hours of Sunday: "*Quam dulcia faucibus meis eloquia tua; super mel ori meo*—How sweet are Thy words unto my taste; yes, sweeter than honey unto my mouth" (Sunday at Sext).

And how imagine the echo in the heart of the contemplative of the single word "Alleluia" or the "Deo Gratias" of the Office? Whether amid the tears of desolation or in the victory and joy of love attained, the contemplative will know how to pronounce these words, either in a steadfast spirit of self-sacrifice or with a smile of enraptured bliss.

II. *The divine Office and the mystery of union with Christ.*

One day during the chant of Matins, St. Mechtilde saw in vision St. John the Evangelist passing through the choir from stall to stall. In his hand he bore a chalice, and "approaching it to the lips of each one of the nuns, he gathered their fervor and their purity of intention in the chant of the psalms, and he offered this precious cup to Jesus who drained it with gladness.'"¹

The contemplative soul is liturgical by instinct. For the more closely one is identified with Christ in the life of prayer, the more deeply is one conscious of being united with Him in the Office in the one same praise of the Father, of being an instrument at His service, by word of mouth and with entire soul and body, and of being one also with all the blessed in heaven who are united with Him in eternal praise.

"Once at Vespers, during the chant of the doxology: 'Jesus, the Virgin-born to Thee; all praise and glory ever be,' St. Gertrude saw in vision a great multitude of blessed spirits hovering above the nuns in choir, and the joyful accents of their sweet song made the vaults re-echo these same words." She wished to know what profit men might derive from this union of the angelic song with the chant of earth. After having renewed her request, she was given to understand "that the heavenly hosts present at the solemnities of the Church militant on earth interceded for the faithful who strove to emulate their devotion and prayed the Most High to grant them true purity of body and soul."²

This constant praise to Jesus in the Office, or to God through Jesus, sustains the soul in the contemplative union without effort on its part. Indeed one may say that the divine Office has a magnetic power of fixing the soul in its relation to Christ.

Throughout the richly patterned fabric of the Office the name of our Lord recurs in many forms, as if the soul could not cease to repeat it: Christ, Redeemer, Prince of

¹*L'Annee liturgique d'apres St. Gertrude et St. Mechtilde*, coll. Pax, t. 1, p. 29.
²*Ibid.*, p. 75.

Peace, the gracious King, the Admirable One, Emmanuel, Savior, Crown of Virgins, etc. St. Bernard voices this devotion in the Matins hymn of the feast of the Holy Name:

> "O Jesus, light of all below,
> Thou fount of life and fire,
> Surpassing all the joys we know,
> And all we can desire.
>
> May every heart confess Thy name,
> And ever Thee adore,
> And seeking Thee, itself inflame
> To seek Thee more and more."

Throughout the course of the Office, Jesus accompanies the mystic soul as He accompanied St. Catherine in church. And each time they came to the doxology, Catherine bowed her head toward Jesus, saying: "Glory be to the Father, and to Thee, and to the Holy Spirit."

Daily at Matins the fifth blessing expresses the wish that "Christ may give us the joys of eternal life." How this phrase must stir the soul of the mystic, whether in the states of aridity or of exile or of union! For to such a soul every phrase of the Office carries its full value.

Daily in the morning hour of Prime occurs the repeated invocation: "Christ, Thou Son of the living God, have mercy on us"; and at night, in Compline, the final wish "that we may watch with Christ and rest in peace."

The Common Offices, especially those of confessors and virgins, keep the image of our Lord ever in the foreground:

> *"Jesu Redemptor omnium,*
> *Perpes corona principum.*

Redeemer blest of all mankind,
Thy pontiffs' endless prize."
>   (Hymn at Lauds, Confessor-pontiff.)

"Jesu, corona celsior,
Et veritas sublimior.

Jesus, eternal truth sublime,
Through endless years the same."
>   (Hymn at Lauds, Confessor-non-pontiff.)

"Jesu, corona virginum,
Qui pergis inter lilia,
Sponsus decorus gratia,
Sponsisque reddens praemium.

Jesus, crown of all the virgin choir,
Amid the lilies Thou art found,
For Thy pure brides with lavish hand
Scatt'ring immortal graces round."
>   (Hymn at Lauds, Virgins.)

With what insight and intimate experience must not the contemplative soul follow the course of the divine Office throughout the cycle of the liturgical year, from the tender joy of the Christmas season to the victory of the risen Christ at Easter and on to the majestic day of His coming at the end of time.

The Advent season has aroused an eager expectation and begs insistently: *"Veni, Domine Jesu*—Come, Lord Jesus." And then in the First Vespers of the Nativity we are told: "When the sun is risen in the heavens, ye shall see the King of kings proceeding forth from the Father as a bridegroom from his chamber" (antiphon at the Magnificat). And at Lauds the fifth antiphon sings: "A little

Child is this day born unto us, and He shall be called God, the Mighty One, alleluia, alleluia."

On the night of the Nativity, at Matins, St. Gertrude continued the exercises which on the preceding evening had brought her so many graces. "Our Lord, to correspond with her movements of fidelity and devotion, drew her entirely to Himself, so that, by a sweet influence of His divinity in her soul, and by a reflux of knowledge which passed from her soul to God, she knew all that was chanted at Matins, whether the responsories or psalms, and this knowledge gave her ineffable and incomprehensible joy. While this continued, she beheld all the saints standing before the throne of the King of kings, reciting Matins with great devotion for His honor and glory."[1]

During the Christmas season the mystic soul enjoys a sweet intimacy with the divine Child and experiences a tender devotion which the Church voices in St. Bernard's hymn:

> "Jesus, the very thought of Thee,
> With sweetness fills my breast;
> But sweeter far Thy face to see,
> And in Thy presence rest."
>
> (First Vespers, Feast of the Holy Name.)

The Office of the Passion has moved the mystics perhaps even more deeply. The soul elevated to the state of spiritual marriage beholds the Bridegroom "coming from Edom," His garments stained with blood, like one who comes forth from the wine press, in which He Himself has been grievously tortured; listens to the daughter of Sion as she weeps in the night with the tears upon her cheeks (Thursday of Holy Week, 1 noct.); shares in the

[1] *The Life and Revelations of St. Gertrude*, London, 1865, p. 308.

"mortal sadness" (3 resp.) and hears the plaintive cry: "O all ye that pass by the way, look and see if there be any sorrow like to my sorrow: for He hath made a vintage of me, as the Lord spoke in the day of His wrath" (1 noct.).

In passing through this dolorous garden the contemplative soul is moved to overflowing love, to an infinite tenderness, desiring to soothe His pain. St. Teresa felt the desire to approach reverently and to wipe away the bloody sweat. The bride unites herself to the Victim and craves to share in the immolation.

"One time," says St. Teresa, "being at Matins, I received a mental illumination, so clear that it seemed an actual picture in my imagination. The Savior came and placed Himself within my arms and upon my knees in the position which we see in the fifth agony (of the Blessed Virgin). I was much frightened at this vision, but Jesus said to me: 'Be not afraid, for My Father is thus united with your soul in a union incomparably more wonderful.'"[1]

The liturgical year moves onward, into the triumphant joy of Easter, the fiery splendor of Pentecost, and the radiant glory of Corpus Christi. The contemplative soul is now all light and strength, and wonderfully expands in love, for the work of redemption has been accomplished, the mystery of life through death, which every true contemplative knows well by personal inward experience, has reached its climax, and the soul rejoices in infinite hope.

"On Easter Monday, when St. Mechtilde heard the words *Mane nobiscum* of the Gospel of the day, she implored the divine Son: 'O sweetest Savior, abide with me I pray you, for the day of my life declines toward its evening.' 'Yes,' replied our Lord, 'I shall remain with you as

[1] *Mercedes de Dios*, t. II, Merced. 58.

a father with his child, as friend with friend, as a bridegroom attends his bride.' "¹

"On Ascension day, during the chant of the responsory *Omnis pulchritudo Domini*, Mechtilde exclaimed with a sigh: 'Alas, my Beloved, Thy beauty, Thy divine charms, are they taken from us?' Jesus replied: 'Indeed they are not taken away; I remain with you with all my grace, with all my power, with full title to the homage of men, with all my glory and all my love. Verily I say to you, I am with you always.' "²

"As the hymn *Veni Creator* was chanted at Terce on Pentecost, our Lord appeared to St. Gertrude and opened wide His heart, full of sweetness and tenderness, to her. Gertrude knelt before Him, inclining her head so that it rested upon His bosom. But the Lord, lifting her head pressed her to Himself, and so united her will to His and sanctified it."³

With what conviction, therefore, of love known by intimate experience, must the contemplative repeat throughout the octave of the feast of Corpus Christi: "*O quam suavis est, Domine, Spiritus tuus*—How sweet, O Lord, is Thy Spirit" (First Vespers, at the *Magnificat*).

III. *The divine Office and contemplation of the mystery of the Holy Trinity.*

Always above the horizon of the divine Office appears the august mystery of the Trinity. Everything recalls it. The very structure of the Office, especially of the Matins hour, constantly suggests it: three nocturns, each containing three psalms, three lessons and three responso-

¹*L'Annee liturgique d'apres St. Gertrude*, 11, p. 124.
²*Ibid.*, 11, p. 157.
³*The Life and Revelations of St. Gertrude*, pp. 417-8.

ries, and three blessings invoking in turn the three divine Persons. At the end of Matins there is the trinitarian hymn, the *Te Deum*. The Minor Hours and Compline have each three psalms and a hymn of three stanzas. Thus the mystic can never lose sight for a moment of the divine presence which is likewise the center of all the soul's interior prayer

Built thus upon a trinitarian foundation, the text of the Office contains many elements apt to stimulate in the contemplative soul acts of faith and love toward the three divine Persons: the Apostles Creed, the *Te Deum*, the Athanasian Creed, the hymn of Terce, the *Gloria Patri* at the end of every psalm.

> "Come, Holy Ghost, who ever one
> Reignest with Father and with Son,
> It is the hour, our souls possess,
> With Thy full flood of holiness."
>
> (Daily at Terce.)

> "Now doth the fiery sun decline,
> Thou, Unity eternal, shine,
> Thou, Trinity, Thy blessings pour,
> And make our hearts with love run o'er."
>
> (Saturday at Vespers.)

In the course of the liturgical year, the soul conducted by Christ ascends by degrees which correspond to the advance of His own earthly life to the summit marked by the feast of the Holy Trinity. Thus the contemplative, "by the love of God seen by men" is brought "to the love of things unseen," to the three divine Persons, the supreme object of the soul's desire. "O the depths of the riches of the wisdom and knowledge of God! How incomprehensible are His judgments, and how unsearchable His ways!" (Chapter of Saturday at Vespers.)

Thus the Office of the feast of the Holy Trinity brings to the mystic a foretaste of heavenly bliss as the First Vespers begins with the majestic antiphon: "Glory be to Thee, O equal Trinity, one Deity, both before all ages and now and forever." And how inviting to contemplation are the lessons of Matins in which the great dogma of the Trinity is set forth in the pure doctrine of St. Fulgentius and St. Gregory Nazianzen.

"On the feast of the effulgent and ever-peaceful Trinity, St. Gertrude recited this salutation: 'Be Thou glorified, O most mighty, most excellent, most noble, most sweet, most benignant ever-peaceful and ineffable Trinity, who art one God now and to endless ages!' As she offered this salutation to our Lord, He appeared to her in His humanity, in which He is said to be less than His Father, and stood in the presence of the adorable Trinity with all the beauty and grace of a perfect man. . . . When Vespers commenced, our Lord offered His heart to the blessed Trinity as a musical instrument, and by it every note and every word which was chanted in the Office on that day resounded most melodiously before God."[1]

"At the antiphon *Osculetur me* a voice came from the throne singing: 'Let My divine Son, in whom is all my delight, approach and embrace Me.' Then the Son of God approached under His human form, embracing this incomprehensible Divinity, to which His sacred humanity alone has merited to be united so blessedly and so inseparably."[2]

"St. Gertrude learned also that whenever the Son is named on this most holy festival, the Father unites Himself in an ineffable manner with the Son, whose humanity receives thereby a glory which reflects upon the saints,

[1] *Ibid.*, p. 421.
[2] *Ibid.*, p. 422.

giving them new knowledge of the incomprehensible Trinity."[1] One may imagine then what faith and admiration are aroused in the contemplative soul at the words of the Office: "The Father is Love, the Son is Grace, the Holy Spirit is Communion; O Blessed Trinity!"

St. Teresa tells us that one day while in choir at the recitation of the Athanasian Creed she suddenly received dazzling revelations concerning the Holy Trinity.[2]

There is in the Breviary this one feast of the Holy Trinity, but truly the Office in all its parts and on all days celebrates this supreme mystery and its homage of praise here on earth is always in close union with the praise of the Holy Trinity in the courts of heaven. "Two Seraphim cried, one to the other: Holy, Holy, Holy." The Church repeats these words in a responsory on all the Sundays after Pentecost, which are also the Sundays after Trinity.

And thus every year, every Sunday, yes, every day, the Church chants the praise of the three divine Persons; indeed, one may say in every hour and at every moment of the divine Office; for to the contemplative each *Gloria Patri* is as a sigh of love for the divine Trinity, a glance toward its dazzling light, an exclamation of joy in token of the soul's complete devotion.

It is obvious that to recite or meditate the Office in such dispositions is to discover in it a fulness of meaning which only the mystics can appreciate. It is only these exalted souls who are able to realize the illimitable scope of this prayer and to recognize all the treasures which it contains. To them the Office is indeed the enraptured breathing of the Bride asleep on the Bridegroom's breast, the incomparable loving union of Christ and His Church.

[1] *Ibid.*, p. 422.
[2] *Vie*, ch. 39.

APPENDIX

OUTLINE OF THE OFFICE

MATINS

Our Father—Hail Mary—Apostles Creed.
v/ Lord, thou shalt open my lips,
r/ And my mouth will announce thy praise.
v/ Incline unto mine aid, O Good.
r/ O Lord, make haste to help me.
Glory be to the Father, etc.

INVITATORY, Ps. 94.

HYMN.

NOCTURNS. in each nocturn:

> THREE PSALMS with antiphons (double or semi-
> Versicle and Response.
> Our Father.
> Absolution.
> Pray, sir, a blessing (before each lesson).
> Blessing.
>
> THREE LESSONS, ending with:
> v/ But thou, O Lord, have mercy on us.
> r/ Thanks be to God.
>
> THREE RESPONSORIES (Glory be to the Father,
>   ing added in the third, sixth and eighth).

TE DEUM.

If Lauds do not follow immediately add:

v/ O Lord, hear my prayer.
r/ And let my cry come unto thee.
PRAYER (same as Collect of the Mass).

v/ O Lord, hear my prayer.
r/ And let my cry come unto thee.
v/ Let us bless the Lord.
r/ Thanks be to God.
May the souls of the faithful departed through the mercy of God rest in peace. Amen.
  Our Father.

LAUDS

Our Father—Hail Mary.
v/ Incline unto mine aid, O God.
r/ O Lord, make haste to help me.
Glory be to the Father, etc.

FIVE PSALMS with antiphons (double or semi-double).

CHAPTER.

HYMN.

Versicle and Response.

THE BENEDICTUS with its antiphon.

v/ O Lord, hear my prayer.
r/ And let my cry come unto thee.

PRAYER (same as Collect of the Mass of the day).

Commemorations (if any).

Prayers (on days when they are prescribed).

v/ O Lord, hear my prayer.
r/ And let my cry come unto thee.
v/ Let us bless the Lord.
r/ Thanks be to God.
May the souls of the faithful departed through the mercy of God rest in peace. Amen.
  Our Father.

Antiphon of the Blessed Virgin (according to the season).

PRIME

Our Father—Hail Mary—Apostles Creed
v/ Incline unto mine aid, O God.
r/ O Lord, make haste to help me.
Glory be to the Father, etc.

HYMN (the last stanza sometimes changed).

Antiphon (always semi-double).
THREE PSALMS (sometimes four).

CHAPTER.

Short Responsory.

Prayers (on days when prescribed).

v/ O Lord, hear my prayer.
r/ And let my cry come unto thee.
Let us pray: O Lord, God almighty, etc.
v/ O Lord, hear my prayer.
r/ And let my cry come unto thee.
v/ Let us bless the Lord.
r/ Thanks be to God.
(Martyrology—when recited in choir).
v/ Precious in the sight of the Lord,
r/ Is the death of his saints.
May holy Mary and all the saints plead for us, etc.
v/ Incline unto mine aid, O God. } (three times)
r/ O Lord, make haste to help me. }
Glory be to the Father, etc.
Lord, have mercy on us, etc.
Our Father.
v/ Look down upon thy servants, etc.
r/ And let the brightness of the Lord, etc.
Glory be to the Father, etc.
Let us pray: O Lord God, King of heaven and earth, e
Pray, Lord, a blessing.
Blessing.
SHORT LESSON (Chapter of None on feast days).
But thou, O Lord, have mercy on us.

v/ Our help is in the name of the Lord.
r/ Who made heaven and earth.
Blessing.
   Our Father.

TERCE—SEXT—NONE

   Our Father—Hail Mary.
v/ Incline unto mine aid, O God.
r/ O Lord, make haste to help me.
Glory be to the Father, etc.

HYMN (last stanza sometimes changed).

Antiphon (semi-double).

THREE PSALMS.

CHAPTER.

Short Responsory.

Prayers (if prescribed).

v/ O Lord, hear my prayer.
r/ And let my cry come unto thee.

PRAYER (as at Lauds and as Collect of the Mass).

v/ O Lord, hear my prayer.
r/ And let my cry come unto thee.
v/ Let us bless the Lord.
r/ Thanks be to God.
May the souls of the faithful departed, etc.
   Our Father.
   Antiphon of the Blessed Virgin (according to the s

VESPERS

   Our Father—Hail Mary.
v/ Incline unto mine aid, O God.
r/ O Lord, make haste to help me.
Glory be to the Father, etc.

Five Psalms with antiphons (double or semi-double).

Chapter.

Hymn.

Versicle and Response.

The Magnificat with its antiphon.

Prayers (on days when prescribed).

v/ O Lord, hear my prayer.
r/ And let my cry come unto thee.

Prayer (as at Lauds and as Collect of the Mass).

Commemorations (if any).

v/ O Lord, hear my prayer.
r/ And let my cry come unto thee.
v/ Let us bless the Lord.
r/ Thanks be to God.
May the souls of the faithful departed, etc.
   Our Father.
   Antiphon of the Blessed Virgin (according to the season)

COMPLINE

Pray, Lord, a blessing.
Blessing.

Short Lesson.

v/ But thou, O Lord, have mercy on us.
r/ Thanks be to God.
v/ Our help is in the name of the Lord.
r/ Who made heaven and earth.
Our Father.
Confiteor.
v/ Convert us, O Lord our savior.
r/ And turn away thine anger from us.
v/ Incline unto mine aid, O God.
r/ O Lord, make haste to help me.
Glory be to the Father, etc.
Antiphon (semi-double).

THREE PSALMS.

HYMN.

CHAPTER.

Short Responsory.

THE NUNC DIMITTIS with its antiphon.
Prayers (when prescribed).

v/ O Lord, hear my prayer.
r/ And let my cry come unto thee.
Let us pray: Visit, we beseech thee, etc.

v/ O Lord, hear my prayer.
r/ And let my cry come unto thee.
v/ Let us bless the Lord.
r/ Thanks be to God.
Blessing.

> Antiphon of the Blessed Virgin (according to the season).
> May the divine assistance remain always with us. Amen.
> Our Father—Hail Mary—Apostles Creed.

General Remarks Regarding the Use of the Breviary

A calendar called the *Ordo* tells what Office is to be said on each day of the year and gives directions for the finding of its parts.

Certain feasts, marked in the Ordo with the letter A, are exceptions to the general rule in that they derive their elements in larger measure from the Proper and less from the Common and follow the plan of the Sunday Office (see the tables below).

In semi-double, simple and ferial Offices the antiphons preceding the psalms are recited only as far as the asterisk (and in full at the end of the psalm). On these same days the Suffrage of the Saints is generally said at Lauds and Vespers; and additional Prayers are said at Prime and Compline (see the rubrics).

A *feria* is a week day on which no feast of a saint occurs.

The last stanza of the hymns is changed on certain days, *e. g.*, on feasts of the Blessed Virgin. Likewise the versicle in the Short Responsory of Prime (see the rubrics).

If commemorations are to be made, these occur in Lauds and Vespers and correspond to the commemorations made in the Mass of the day.

Sample Outlines

We give on the following pages and in tabular form examples of the various types of Offices.

I. SUNDAY OFFICE

	From the Psalter	*From the Season*
Matins	Invitatory Hymn Nine Psalms with their Antiphons } in three Nocturns Versicles and Responses	Nine Lessons with their Responsories for the three Nocturns
Lauds	Psalms and their Antiphons Chapter Hymn Vers. and Resp.	Antiphon for the Benedictus Prayer
Prime	The entire Hour	
Terce Sext None	The entire Hour except	Prayer
Vespers	Psalms and Antiphons Chapter Hymn Vers. and Resp.	Antiphon for the Magficat Prayer
Compline	The entire Hour	

II. FERIAL OR WEEK DAY OFFICE

(Any week day not a saint's day)

	From the Psalter	*From the Season*
Matins	Invitatory Hymn Nine consecutive Psalms with their Antiphons One Vers. and Resp.	Three Lessons with their Responsories in one Nocturn
Lauds	Psalms and Antiphons Chapter Hymn Vers. and Resp. Antiphon for the Benedictus	Prayer (as of the preceding Sunday)
Prime	The entire Hour	
Terce Sext None	The entire Hour except	Prayer (as of the preceding Sunday)
Vespers	Psalms and Antiphons Chapter Hymn Vers. and Resp. Antiphon for the Magnificat	Prayer (as of the preceding Sunday)
Compline	The entire Hour	

III. AN "A" (Exceptional) FEAST
(e.g., September 8, the Nativity of the Blessed Virgin)

	From the Psalter	*From the Proper of Saints*	*From the Common of the Bl. Virgin*
I Vespers		Antiphons Vers. & Resp. Antiphon for the Magnificat Prayer	Psalms Chapter Hymn
Matins		Invitatory Lessons and Responsories for the three Nocturns	Hymn Psalms and Antiphons Vers. & Resp. for the three Nocturns
Lauds	Psalms of Sunday	Antiphons Vers. & Resp. Antiphon for the Benedictus Prayer Commemoration	Chapter Hymn
Prime	Psalms of Sunday (as on feasts)	First Antiphon of Lauds	Versicle of the Short Resp.
Terce Sext None	Psalms of Sunday	Second, Third & Fifth Antiphons of Lauds	Chapter Responsory Vers. & Resp.
II Vespers	Same arrangement as for I Vespers		
Compline	of Sunday		

IV. A "B" FEAST OF DOUBLE RANK
(e.g., January 27, the feast of St. John Chrysostom)

	From the Psalter	From the Proper of Season	From the Proper of Saints	From the Common (Conf. Pont.)
I Vespers	Psalms and Antiphons of the day of the week		Prayer Commemoration	Chapter Hymn Vers. & Resp. Antiphon for the Magnificat
Matins	Psalms and Antiphons Versicle and Response of the day of the week	Lessons and Responsories of the first Nocturn	Lessons and Responsories of the second Nocturn	Invitatory Hymn Lessons (Homily) and Responsories of third Nocturn
Lauds	Psalms and Antiphons of the day of the week		Prayer	Chapter Hymn Vers. & Resp. Antiphon for the Benedictus
Prime	Psalms and Antiphons of the day of the week and the rest			Short Lesson
Terce Sext None	Psalms and Antiphons of the day of the week		Prayer	Chapter Short Responsory Vers. & Resp.
II Vespers	Psalms and Antiphons of the day of the week		Prayer Commemoration	Chapter Hymn Vers. & Resp. Antiphon for the Magnificat
Compline	of the day of the week			

V. A "B" FEAST OF SEMI-DOUBLE RANK

(*e.g.*, August 25, the feast of St. Louis)

	From the Psalter	*From the Proper* of Season of Saints	*From the Common*
Matins Lauds etc.			

Same arrangement as for a "B" feast of double rank, but in addition:

At Lauds the Suffrage of the Saints is said (Ant., V.R., Prayer).

At Prime the extra Prayers as on Sunday.

At Vespers the Suffrage of the Saints (unless the following day is a double).

At Compline the extra Prayers.

VI. A SIMPLE FEAST

(*e.g.*, October 26, the feast of St. Evaristus)

	From the Psalter	*From the Proper* of Season of Saints	*From the Common*
Matins Lauds etc.			

Same arrangement as for a "B" feast of semi-double rank, except: At Matins the nine psalms (of the day in the psalter) are said consecutively (as in a ferial Office) and are followed by three lessons, of which the first and second are taken from the Proper of the Season and the third (followed by the *Te Deum*) is taken from the Proper of the Saints.

www.ingramcontent.com/pod-product-compliance
Ingram Content Group UK Ltd.
Pitfield, Milton Keynes, MK11 3LW, UK
UKHW041945230426
12048UKWH00008B/136